THE GEEKY CHEF DRINKS

Unofficial Cocktail Recipes from Game of Thrones, Legend of Zelda, Star Trek, and More

Dedicated to my grandfather, Roger Reeder,

who had his first drink of beer in his fifties and declared it had potential.

Brimming with creative inspiration, how-to projects, and useful information to enrich your everyday life, Quarto Knows is a favorite destination for those pursuing their interests and passions. Visit our site and dig deeper with our books into your area of interest: Quarto Creates, Quarto Cooks, Quarto Homes, Quarto Lives, Quarto Drives, Quarto Explores, Quarto Gifts, or Quarto Kids.

First published in 2018 by Race Point Publishing, an imprint of The Quarto Group, 142 West 36th Street, 4th Floor, New York, NY 10018, USA

T (212) 779-4972 F (212) 779-6058 www.QuartoKnows.com

Race Point Publishing titles are also available at discount for retail, wholesale, promotional, and bulk purchase. For details, contact the Special Sales Manager by email at specialsales@quarto.com or by mail at The Quarto Group, Attn: Special Sales Manager, 401 Second Avenue North, Suite 310, Minneapolis, MN 55401, USA.

10 9 8 7 6 5 4 3 2 1

ISBN: 978-1-63106-560-6

Library of Congress Cataloging-in-Publication Data is available

Cover and interior illustrations by Denis Caron
Photographer: Bill Milne
Editorial Director: Jeannine Dillon
Managing Editor: Erin Canning
Project Editor: Melanie Madden
Cover and Interior Design: Rosamund Saunders

Printed in China

THE GEEKY CHEF DRINKS

Unofficial Cocktail Recipes from Game of Thrones, Legend of Zelda, Star Trek, and More

Cassandra Reeder, The Geeky Chef

Race Point
PUBLISHING

CONTENTS

Crafting

INTRODUCTION

Since, well, birth, but more publicly since I started *The Geeky Chef* in 2008, my passion project has been making recipes for fictional or unusual foods from books, TV, movies, and games. I don't know if it's the tendency of us writers to, well, let's say, have a disposition towards alcoholism, but a whole lot of these foods tend to be alcoholic beverages. Enough to fill a whole book of their own. This book, actually.

The bad news is: I'm not a mixologist. I'm not Guinan or Quark. I'm definitely not Sam Malone. I'm not even Tom Cruise, though I am his height and much less likely to sue you. That being said, I have had some practice at drink-making over the years as The Geeky Chef. I actually learned a lot just making this book. So, the good news is: If I can learn to make a decent cocktail, you absolutely can, too! These are cocktails for geeky laymen by a geeky lay … man. The other good news is: I have some friends (I know, it's a miracle I have friends at all!) who are also bartenders, and they gave me some great cocktail wisdom, a burden I now pass on to you, Padawan.

I will try to keep things as simple as possible, but I do recommend these five things:

1 **Get a cocktail shaker.** I cannot stress this one enough: The use of a cocktail shaker can improve a cocktail by approximately 1,000 percent! Mixing glasses can be sort of improvised, but the mystical effects of a cocktail shaker can't be understated. There's a reason James Bond likes his martinis shaken …

2 **Embrace the bitters.** Outside of the bartending world, unsavvy folks like you and me may not understand the power and appeal of bitters. I'm here to tell you, they are like the seasoning of drinks, the final incantation that makes the potion fully effective. Don't be afraid of the "bitter" in the name; most of them aren't even particularly bitter. They're called bitters because the essence of their flavor is distilled from their ingredients, sort of like The Force being distilled into a sprinkle-ready bottle.

3 **Use simple syrups.** This is the best way to sweeten a cocktail, period. Adding a touch of sweetness and flavor, they easily dissolve into liquids and can vastly improve any cocktail.

4 **Adjust ratios to your liking!** If you like a stiff drink, bump up the alcohol or reduce the mixers. If you like a mellower drink, lower the alcohol amounts and/or increase the non-alcoholic ingredients. If you like a sweeter drink, just increase the amount of

syrup, soda, or juice. Despite what some may have you believe, crafting cocktails is not an objective science. You won't have Professor Snape slapping your hand if you don't add exactly three drops of dragon blood while stirring counterclockwise for five and a half turns, I promise.

5 **Buy like the smarty-pants nerd you are.** Unlike my previous books, I couldn't completely avoid expensive or unusual ingredients. Alcohol is just *not cheap*. I did avoid naming specific brands whenever possible, but sometimes I had to cite specific products for their unique color, flavor, or effects. My advice is, buy the stuff you like in bulk at warehouse clubs, and if you're not sure you're going to like it, buy the little mini bottles. Those little guys usually run to $1 to $4 for about 50 ml of liquid—and they make great potion bottles later!

1
SIMPLE SYRUPS

Classic Simple Syrup

Fruit Syrups: **GRENADINE, BERRY**

Herbal Syrups: **LAVENDER, GINGER, CINNAMON**

Other Syrups: **HONEY, BROWN SUGAR, SPICED MAPLE**

It's all in the name. Simple syrups are just that: simple. Simple to make, simple to use, and once you get the hang of them you can easily make your own magical concoctions. Lavender honey syrup? Yes! Blueberry cinnamon syrup? Go for it! Here are some of my favorites to get you started.

⚜ STERILIZING TIP ⚜

It's best to store simple syrups in airtight, sterilized storage containers (a thick glass bottle or jar with a lid works best). The easiest way to do this is to use the dishwasher's high temperature setting. No dishwasher? Here are some instructions on how to sterilize heat-resistant glassware:

1 Place the glass container(s) right side up in a canner or a deep pot with a rack at the bottom.
2 Fill the canner or pot with water until it is 1 inch (2.5 cm) above the container(s).
3 Bring the water to a boil over medium-high heat and continue to boil for approximately 10 minutes.
4 Reduce the heat and keep the container(s) in the hot water until you're ready to fill with syrup.
5 Remove from the hot water carefully with protective gloves and/or tongs.

CLASSIC SIMPLE SYRUP

1 cup (200 g) granulated sugar
1 cup (235 ml) water

1 In a saucepan, combine the sugar and water.

2 Bring to a boil and cook over a medium heat, stirring regularly, until the sugar has dissolved, about 3-5 minutes.

3 Allow to cool before storing in an airtight storage container.

FRUIT SYRUPS

There are basically two ways to make fruit syrups: you can begin with either fresh fruit or fruit juice. You can substitute different kinds of fruit in the blueberry syrup for a different flavor, although berries work best. I like raspberries and strawberries myself. Likewise, you can substitute any kind of juice in the grenadine recipe, including cherry or pineapple.

 STORAGE TIP

Add 1 tablespoon (15 ml) of vodka to the syrups after
they are prepared to make them last longer in storage. They
usually keep for about a month in the refrigerator.

GRENADINE

Most of us are familiar with grenadine as the red, artificially flavored, candy-like cherry syrup you get at diners and soda shops, but originally grenadine was made using fresh pomegranate. I'm not saying you have it make it from scratch, but I *will* say you *should*, because your taste buds will throw you a party.

1 cup (235 ml) pomegranate juice
  (preferably one without added
  sugar)
¾ cup (150 g) granulated sugar
1 teaspoon fresh lemon juice
2–3 drops of orange flower water

1 Mix the pomegranate juice and sugar in a small saucepan and cook over a medium-low heat, stirring, until the sugar has completely dissolved.

2 Bring the heat down to low and continue to cook, stirring occasionally, until the mixture has thickened, about 20 minutes. Remove from the heat and stir in the lemon juice and orange flower water.

3 Let cool to around room temperature before storing in a sterilized airtight container.

BERRY SYRUP

1 cup (100 g) frozen or fresh
blueberries, blackberries,
strawberries, or raspberries
1 cup (235 ml) water
½ cup (100 g) granulated sugar
1 teaspoon lemon zest

1 Add all the ingredients to a saucepan and bring the liquid to a boil.

2 Reduce the heat to low and simmer for 15 minutes.

3 While still hot, pour through a mesh strainer into a sterilized, airtight, heat-resistant storage container.

4 Let the syrup cool to around room temperature before using or capping the container.

HERBAL SYRUPS

I love to use herbal syrups in my baking and cooking, but especially in my drinking. The great thing is, the method is pretty much always the same, though some herbs or spices may need additional "steeping" time if you want a strong flavor.

LAVENDER SYRUP

3 tablespoons dried lavender buds
(culinary grade) or 3 lavender
tea bags
1 cup (235 ml) water
1½ cups (300 g) granulated sugar

1 Add the lavender to the water in a saucepan and bring to a boil, then stir in the sugar and cook until it's fully dissolved, 3–5 minutes, stirring occasionally.

2 Reduce the heat to low and simmer for about 15 minutes.

3 Remove from the heat and allow to cool and steep for 45 minutes.

4 Strain the syrup into a sterilized airtight container.

GINGER SYRUP

¾ cup (75 g) peeled and sliced
  fresh ginger
1 cup (235 ml) water
1½ cups (300 g) granulated sugar

1 Add the ginger to the water in a saucepan and bring to a boil, then stir in the sugar and cook until it's fully dissolved, stirring occasionally.

2 Reduce the heat to low and simmer for about 15 minutes.

3 Remove from the heat and allow to cool to around room temperature, as the ginger infuses the syrup.

4 Strain the syrup into a sterilized airtight container.

CINNAMON SYRUP

5 cinnamon sticks
1 cup (235 ml) water
1 cup (200 g) granulated sugar

1 Add the cinnamon sticks to the water in a saucepan and bring to a boil, then stir in the sugar and cook until it's fully dissolved, stirring occasionally.

2 Reduce the heat to low and simmer for about 15 minutes.

3 Remove from the heat and allow to cool and steep for 45 minutes.

4 Strain the syrup into a sterilized airtight container.

OTHER SYRUPS

HONEY SYRUP

¾ cup (175 ml) water
¾ cup (255 g) honey

1 Add the water and honey to a saucepan.

2 Heat over a medium-high heat, stirring occasionally, until the honey dissolves into the water, but don't boil.

3 Let cool to around room temperature before storing the syrup in a sterilized airtight container.

BROWN SUGAR SYRUP

1 cup (235 ml) water
1½ cups (340 g) dark brown sugar
1 teaspoon vanilla extract

1 Add the water and brown sugar to a saucepan and bring to a boil, stirring regularly.

2 Reduce the heat to low and continue stirring until all the sugar has dissolved.

3 Remove from the heat and stir in the vanilla.

4 Let cool to room temperature before storing the syrup in a sterilized airtight container.

SPICED MAPLE SYRUP

½ cup (170 g) real maple syrup
½ cup (120 ml) water
2 whole allspice
2 cinnamon sticks
2 whole cloves
2 star anise

1   Add the maple syrup, water, and all the spices to a small saucepan.

2   Bring to a boil and then turn off the heat.

3   Cover the pan and let the syrup cool and steep for 45 minutes.

4   Strain the syrup into a sterilized airtight container.

2
SPECIAL EFFECTS

—◇—

Rimming the Glass: **SUGARED/SALTED RIM, SPARKLY RIM, CANDY RIM**

THE SKEWER

Ice Effects: **SHAPE, COLOR, GARNISH**

THE SPIRAL CITRUS PEEL

THE SHIMMER EFFECT

THE MIST EFFECT

Playing with Fire: **THE FLAMING FLOAT, THE CITRUS FLAME**

We're making magical and high-tech drinks here, and sometimes they need to look more, well, magical and high-tech. How or whether to garnish is totally up to you, but here are some impressive ways to decorate a drink. With special effects, you can choose just one, or use multiple effects for a very impressive-looking drink!

RIMMING THE GLASS

This always needs to be done before the drink is prepared.

SUGARED/SALTED RIM

This is a classic. Any type of sugar or salt can be used, but as a rule you don't want to pick one that's super fine or super coarse. You can also purchase cocktail rimming sugars and salts, which have been crafted with the intention of being used to rim cocktail glasses and come in a variety of flavors and colors.

HOW TO RIM A GLASS:

1 Add sugar or salt to a shallow dish.

2 Moisten the rim of the serving glass. (Water works fine in most cases.)

3 Dip the glass into the salt or sugar.

4 If you want more sugar or salt on the rim, slightly twist the glass.

HOW TO COLOR SUGAR OR SALT:

1 Put ¼ cup (50 g) of sugar or salt in a small, sealable plastic bag.

2 Add a drop of food coloring.

3 Seal the plastic bag and shake for a few seconds.

4 If the color is too light, add another drop of food coloring and repeat step 3.

SPARKLY RIM

If you want to add some glitz and glitter, this is a great way to bedazzle your cocktail. Edible glitter can be purchased in the baking section of most grocery stores, at a baking store, or online. I used the Wilton brand, but CK Products are also popular.

Edible glitter (any color)
A little light corn syrup or honey

TIP

For a thicker coat, twist the glass.

1 Place the edible glitter in a shallow bowl or dish that the top of your glass will fit into.

2 Use a pastry brush (or your finger if you don't mind getting sticky) to apply the corn syrup or honey around the rim of the glass. You could also squeeze a ring of corn syrup or honey onto a dish and dip the glass into it.

3 Dip the sticky rim of the glass into the edible glitter or sugar to coat.

Voilà! You have an impressive-looking drink with little to no effort.

CANDY RIM

1 cup (200 g) granulated sugar
½ cup (120 ml) light corn syrup
½ cup (120 ml) water
Candy thermometer
Food coloring (any color)

TIP

It can be a bit difficult to remove the candy from the glass after it hardens, but soaking it in soapy hot water for a half hour or so should loosen it.

1 Combine the sugar, syrup, and water in a heavy-bottomed pot over medium-high heat, and pop in the candy thermometer. Don't stir until the liquid reaches 300°F (150°C).

2 Once heated to 300°F (150°C), remove the thermometer and stir in the food coloring, making sure the color is evenly mixed in.

3 Dip the heatproof serving glass into the mixture while it's still hot, then turn it upright, being careful not to let any syrup get on you. The syrup will drip down the glass and then harden for a drippy effect.

THE SKEWER

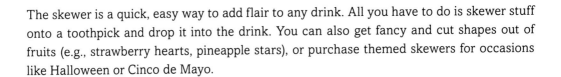

The skewer is a quick, easy way to add flair to any drink. All you have to do is skewer stuff onto a toothpick and drop it into the drink. You can also get fancy and cut shapes out of fruits (e.g., strawberry hearts, pineapple stars), or purchase themed skewers for occasions like Halloween or Cinco de Mayo.

> ### 🍸 TIP 🍸
>
> Make sure to skewer stuff with flavors or colors that complement the cocktail. You don't want to add a pickle skewer to a Shirley Temple. Or maybe you do!

ICE EFFECTS

Altering the appearance of ice is another easy way to add flair to a drink.

SHAPE

For most cocktails, ice cubes or spheres are best for taste because their melt rate is consistent. However, some more concentrated drinks, like the Mint Julep, benefit from faster-melting crushed or cracked ice. You can also use fun molds to make ice that jibes with the drink's theme. There are all kinds out there: stars, leaves, skulls, etc. I've even seen Tardis, Starfleet, and R2-D2 molds!

COLOR

An easy way to add color or flavor to any drink is to make ice cubes with fruit juice or food dye. If the recipe calls for orange juice, go ahead and freeze some orange juice in ice trays and add it to the drink. Food dyes can be added to regular water and frozen if you just want a color effect. These look especially cool in clear or light-colored drinks.

GARNISH

Freezing fruit, herbs, edible flowers, or any other edible garnish is another easy and impressive way to add a nice visual element to any drink. For this method, you need to boil distilled water, then let it cool before pouring the water into an ice mold and adding the garnish. Boiling the water first allows you to make an ice cube that is more transparent and less cloudy.

THE SPIRAL CITRUS PEEL

Citrus fruits are probably the most common drink garnishes. Most of the time, all you have to do is cut out a slice and drop it in the drink, but you can also cut them into shapes. My favorite citrus garnish is a peel twist. A lot of folks will tell you that you need to peel the citrus fruit a certain way to get the right shape, but that's just not true.

A small citrus fruit (e.g., lemon, tangerine, lime)
A sharp knife

  TIP

For tighter twists, drop the peel into a glass of ice water immediately after creating the spiral.

1 Take your fruit and cut out a round slice from near the center. The slice should be about ¼ inch (6mm) thick.

2 Cut out the center of the slice, removing as much pith (i.e., the white stuff on the inside of the rind) as you can without cutting through the peel itself.

3 Once the pulp and most of the pith is removed, use the knife to cut the circular peel so that it is one long strip.

4 Use your fingers to roll the peel strip into as tight a spiral as you can without breaking it.

THE SHIMMER EFFECT

Edible "luster dust" can be used to add sparkle and shimmer to frostings, gum paste, and fondant. Luckily for us, it can be used in beverages, too!. This shimmery liqueur will add some magic to any cocktail or potion without changing the flavor too much. You can make your own sparkly concoctions by combining any clear liquor you plan to use in your cocktail with any flavor of simple syrup and any color of luster dust!

1 cup (235 ml) clear liquor, such as vodka, white rum, or gin
½ cup (170 ml) Classic Simple Syrup (page 10)
Pinch or 2 of edible luster dust

1 In a small mixing bowl, stir the liquor and simple syrup together with a whisk until the syrup has completely dissolved, about 3 minutes.

2 Gradually whisk in the luster dust.

3 Use a funnel to pour the mixture into a glass bottle. Store in the refrigerator for up to 2 weeks.

4 Swirl the bottle to activate the luster dust before using it in a cocktail.

  TIP

You can find edible luster dust in the baking section near the cake decorations in some grocery stores, in any baking store, and online. Amazon carries a few brands like Wilton, CK Products, and Bakell at reasonable prices.

THE MIST EFFECT

Dry ice adds a bit of mystery to any special brew.

SUPPLIES

Dry ice
Towel or other thick fabric
Safety goggles or other eye
   protection (recommended)
Hammer
Flat-head screwdriver (or something
   that can be used as a chisel)
Thick rubber gloves (recommended)
Tongs
Serving vessel(s)

1 Carefully place the dry ice on the towel and sort of bunch up the towel around it, making sure you do not touch the ice directly. Use the towel to pick up the ice then flip it over onto your work surface.

2 Put on goggles or other eye protection. Use the hammer and screwdriver like a chisel to carefully break up the dry ice into smaller cubes. The size of the cubes depends on whether you are using the ice in the serving glasses directly or in a larger container (like a punch bowl).

3 Use tongs to drop a cube into your serving vessel(s) right before you pour in your drink of choice.

 TIP

Purchase the dry ice a couple hours before planned use, at most. Standard freezers are not cold enough to maintain dry ice. It will melt.

FOR YOUR SAFETY

1 Go full mad scientist and equip yourself with safety goggles or other eye protection and thick rubber gloves.

2 NEVER CONSUME OR DIRECTLY TOUCH DRY ICE, even after it has been added to the cocktail. It can be very dangerous and even cause frostbite. Make sure everyone consuming your beverages knows this.

PLAYING WITH FIRE

FOR YOUR SAFETY

1 Fire and drinking are not the best of friends, so make sure you're sober when attempting to light a drink. You do NOT want to end up like VADER WITHOUT THE SUIT!!!!

2 NEVER drink a cocktail that is currently lit. Wait for the flame to die or snuff it out yourself.

3 DO NOT attempt to blow out the flame. This only spreads the fire.

4 ALWAYS make sure the glass, your hands, the counter, the lighter, and anything else you don't want to set on fire have no alcohol on them. In fact, it's best to remove anything flammable from your prep area.

5 DO NOT use a thin cup or glass; it could shatter from the heat.

6 DO NOT use a plastic cup or a plastic straw if lighting a drink.

7 Sometimes the fire is hard to see, especially if you're in an area with a lot of light. If you've lit the drink and you don't see flames, try turning down the lights. ALWAYS assume the drink is lit and treat it with care.

THE FLAMING FLOAT

SUPPLIES

A cocktail
Thick, heatproof glass
Any 151-proof liquor
Tablespoon
Utility lighter
Fire extinguisher

1 Prepare your cocktail and pour it into the glass. Make sure that there is 1–2 inches (2.5–5 cm) of space below the rim.

2 Once your cocktail is properly prepared, pour some of the high-proof liquor into the tablespoon. Gently spoon the liquor over the drink so it creates a separate top layer.

3 Use the utility lighter to light the alcohol on top of the drink. Stand back and admire, take pictures, etc.

CAUTION

Make sure the fire is extinguished before putting the cup near your face. Flames usually burn out in a minute or so.

THE CITRUS FLAME

This is a garnish that's more about flavor than style—at least after the trick is done. The act of flaming the citrus is pretty stylish, though, so you'll probably get some "oohs" and "ahhs."

SUPPLIES

Paring knife
Fresh citrus fruit (usually an orange)
Utility lighter or match
A cocktail

CAUTION

Be prepared for a burst of flame when the oil from the peel makes contact with the fire.

1 With the paring knife, cut out a 2–3-inch (5–7-cm) piece of citrus peel, trying not to get too much pith.

2 With your lighter or match, hold the flame a few inches (5–7 cm) above the drink.

3 Squeeze the peel over the flame, with the outside of the peel facing down. You'll want to squeeze hard enough to extract enough oil from the peel.

4 Drop the peel into the drink as a garnish.

3
OTHERWORLDLY INTOXICANTS

WHITE-GOLD TOWER

INSPIRED BY **THE ELDER SCROLLS**

Skyrim, I just can't quit you. Every *Elder Scrolls* game is a triumph, but *Skyrim* is the only one I've picked up again four times in seven years and done something completely new every single time. Some things just get better with time. Like *Skyrim*. And alcohol. *Skyrim* had its fair share of alcoholic drinks for your Dragonborn to find or purchase; the most intriguing of these were Talen-Jei's cocktails at The Bee and Barb in Riften. The White-Gold Tower was described as a layered drink containing blended mead, heavy cream, and lavender. It was then topped with Dragon's Tongue, which is a kind of flower in *Skyrim*. This recipe blends two kinds of mead, lavender syrup, and bitters, and tops it off with heavy cream and an edible flower.

SERVES 1

2 fl oz (60 ml) dry mead
2 fl oz (60 ml) Cyser mead
½ fl oz/1 tablespoon (15 ml) whiskey
 (optional)
4–6 dashes of lavender bitters
1 teaspoon Lavender Syrup (page 12)
Ice cubes
1 fl oz (30 ml) heavy cream

1 In a cocktail shaker, combine both meads, whiskey (if using), bitters, syrup, and 2–3 ice cubes. Shake well.

2 Pour the mead mixture into your serving glass.

3 Pour one-third of the heavy cream out of the carton and set aside (you can pour it back in later). Shake the heavy cream carton vigorously for about 30 seconds.

4 Get a spoon and hold it upside down above the mead in the glass, tilted slightly downward. Slowly pour the heavy cream onto the back of the spoon so it indirectly spills over into the glass on top of the mead. It's important not to do this too quickly if you want a layered effect.

SUGGESTED GARNISH:

Edible flower (nasturtium blossoms, orchids, and viola flowers look the most like Dragon Tongue)

SUGGESTED SERVING VESSEL:

Highball glass

VELVET LECHANCE

INSPIRED BY **THE ELDER SCROLLS**

Velvet LeChance, also sold at The Bee and Barb, was described as having blackberries, honey, spiced wine, and a touch of *nightshade*. I went for a pretty literal interpretation of the drink because it already sounds pretty amazing. I know the nightshade they are referring to is the deadly flower, but, luckily for us, the term nightshade could refer to potatoes, paprika, and eggplant, which are all in the nightshade family (although perhaps not the best cocktail ingredients …). I thought the best nightshade to add to this drink was cayenne pepper, to give it a bite.

SERVES 1

5 blackberries
1–2 teaspoons Honey Syrup
 (page 14)
2 fl oz (60 ml) Crème de Mûre
 (blackberry liqueur)
4 fl oz (120 ml) bottled spiced/
 mulled wine (or see Mulled Wine
 recipe on page 120)
Tiny pinch of cayenne pepper

1 In the serving cup, gently muddle the blackberries with the syrup.

2 Pour in the Crème de Mûre, top with the wine, and stir to combine.

3 Top with a tiny pinch of cayenne pepper to serve.

SUGGESTED EFFECTS/GARNISHES:

The Skewer (page 20) with blackberries
The Mist Effect (page 25)

 **TIP**

New to muddling?
Here's how: Press
the berries into the
bottom of the glass with
a "muddler" or wooden
spoon, while twisting
your wrist, for
10–15 seconds.

CHASIND SACK MEAD

INSPIRED BY **DRAGON AGE**

If you have a tendency to develop unhealthy attachments to video-game characters, this game is an enabler. BioWare's *Dragon Age: Inquisition* was a much-anticipated continuation of a beloved fantasy RPG series. The spirits in this game were not consumables, but rather collectibles that you could view in the cellar of Skyhold, the base of operations throughout most of the game. They all had delightfully droll descriptions, which made them fun to collect. Although I was mightily tempted by "Dragon Piss," I chose Chasind Sack Mead because the description was maybe the most, well, descriptive. It involved warm summer days, apple blossoms, honey, and soul-crushing bitterness.

SERVES 1

3 fl oz (90 ml) dry mead
2 fl oz (60 ml) apple whiskey
1 fl oz (30 ml) Bärenjäger or other honey liqueur
1 teaspoon orange blossom water
10–15 dashes of apple bitters, or to taste
Ice cubes

1 Put all the ingredients in a cocktail shaker.

2 Shake, shake, shake!

3 Strain into a serving vessel.

SUGGESTED SERVING VESSELS:

Wine glass
Mug

SUGGESTED GARNISHES:

The Spiral Citrus Peel (page 22) with orange
Honeycomb

THE YELLOW FAIRY

INSPIRED BY **FABLE II**

Microsoft Game Studio's *Fable II* is a game with an unprecedented amount of choices, including drinking yourself into a stupor, purchasing property, and getting married (probably in that order and probably all in one night). The alcoholic drinks in *Fable II* had amusing punny names, granted skill points, and were a great gift for your angry and neglected spouse(s). The Yellow Fairy, a play on "The Green Fairy" (aka absinthe), was one of two five-star drinks in the base game, meaning it was a quality item. It seemed to lend itself best to a cocktail interpretation. The in-game description is that it tastes like marshmallows and may cause liver damage. This is a very strong, bright yellow cocktail with a hint of marshmallow flavor.

SERVES 1

1½ fl oz (45 ml) whipped cream or
    vanilla vodka
1 fl oz (30 ml) overproof white rum
½ fl oz/1 tablespoon of amaretto
    liqueur
2 fl oz (60 ml) pineapple juice
1 tablespoon (15 ml) fresh
    lemon juice
1–2 teaspoons Brown Sugar Syrup
    (page 14)
Ice cubes

1   Add all the liquid ingredients to a cocktail shaker with a few ice cubes.

2   Shake until chilled.

3   Strain into a small bottle or a glass.

SUGGESTED SERVING VESSELS:

Cork bottle
Glass mug

SUGGESTED GARNISHES:

Dollop of Marshmallow Fluff
The Spiral Citrus Peel (page 22) with lemon

NOBLE PURSUIT

INSPIRED BY **THE LEGEND OF ZELDA**

This long-awaited game was everything Zelda fans wanted and more, boasting a giant world with multiple unique regions. In the desert region, Link will happen upon a Gerudo named Pokki, inconveniently languishing on top of the Misae Suma Shrine's door-opening pedestal. Pokki will tell Link that she's dying of thirst and that only a specific drink, the "Noble Pursuit" from The Noble Canteen in Gerudo Town, will save her. Thus begins the quest, "The Perfect Drink," which involves a Gerudo disguise, underage bar-going, and a giant ice cube. For this drink I used two real-world counterparts to in-game ingredients that have a cool or heat-resistant effect: Hydromelons (watermelons) and Cool Safflina (lavender). It really is the perfect drink.

SERVES 2-3

3 cups (450 g) cubed fresh
  watermelon
2 fl oz (60 ml) cold water
2 fl oz (60 ml) light rum
2 fl oz (60 ml) gin
4 teaspoons Lavender Syrup
  (page 12), or to taste
Juice of 1 lime
½ cup ice cubes

1 In a blender, blend the watermelon until smooth.

2 Strain the watermelon through a fine sieve into a pitcher, discarding the pulp.

3 Add the remaining ingredients to the pitcher and stir.

4 Pour into 2–3 glasses.

SUGGESTED EFFECTS/GARNISHES:

The Mist Effect (page 25)
Ice with lavender buds (page 21)
Sprig of lavender

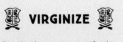

VIRGINIZE

Omit the rum and gin,
adding ½ cup (75 g)
chopped watermelon
and 2 fl oz (60 ml) water.

SULFURON SLAMMER

INSPIRED BY **WORLD OF WARCRAFT**

Blizzard's *World of Warcraft* is the most-played MMORPG of all time. I would know, I spent most of my free time in Azeroth from 2006 to 2007. There are many alcoholic consumables in *WoW*. SO MANY. I wanted to choose drinks that had something special going, like the Sulfuron Slammer. The item description says it is an extremely potent flaming alcoholic beverage: "It'll knock your socks off … and then set your feet on fire." Like most alcohols in *WoW*, this one can cause blurred vision and cockiness, but it'll also literally set you on fire. Spicy, sweet, and the color of sulfur, thish drink ish … Hic! What was I saying?

SERVES 1

2 fl oz (60 ml) gold tequila
1 fl oz (30 ml) Ancho Reyes
½ fl oz (15 ml) amaretto
2 fl oz (60 ml) pineapple juice
2–3 dashes of Angostura bitters
Ice cubes

1 Add all the liquid ingredients to a cocktail shaker with 2–3 ice cubes. Shake well.

2 Strain into a serving glass.

SUGGESTED EFFECT/GARNISH:

The Flaming Float (page 28)
Jalapeño slices

MOONGLOW

INSPIRED BY **WORLD OF WARCRAFT**

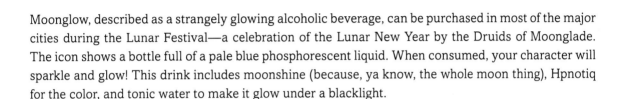

Moonglow, described as a strangely glowing alcoholic beverage, can be purchased in most of the major cities during the Lunar Festival—a celebration of the Lunar New Year by the Druids of Moonglade. The icon shows a bottle full of a pale blue phosphorescent liquid. When consumed, your character will sparkle and glow! This drink includes moonshine (because, ya know, the whole moon thing), Hpnotiq for the color, and tonic water to make it glow under a blacklight.

SERVES 1

¾ fl oz (22 ml) moonshine
2 fl oz (60 ml) Hpnotiq liqueur
¼ tablespoon fresh lemon juice
1 teaspoon Classic Simple Syrup
  (page 10)
Ice cubes
3 fl oz (90 ml) tonic water

1   In a mixing glass, stir together the moonshine, Hpnotiq, lemon juice, and simple syrup, along with a few ice cubes.

2   Pour the contents of the mixing glass into the serving glass or bottle.

3   Top with tonic water and stir.

4   Turn on a blacklight.

5   Douse yourself with glitter. Or don't.

SUGGESTED SERVING VESSEL:

Round cork bottle

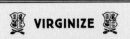 **VIRGINIZE**

Omit the moonshine
and replace the Hpnotiq
with blue Hawaiian
Punch or similar.

4
MAGICAL ELIXIRS

Grimm: **AMOR DI INFIERNO**

Fantastic Beasts and Where to Find Them: **GIGGLE WATER**

The Legend of Zelda: **CHATEAU ROMANI**

Final Fantasy: **HERO DRINK**

The Lord of the Rings: **MIRUVOR**

Your Favorite Video Game: **RED POTION**

Your Favorite Video Game: **BLUE POTION**

Your Favorite Video Game: **GREEN POTION**

AMOR DI INFIERNO

INSPIRED BY GRIMM

Grimm is a fantasy police procedural that follows Nick, a homicide detective who finds out that he is a descendent of a line of supernatural hunters called "Grimms." Grimms are responsible for keeping the balance between humanity and supernatural entities known as "Wesen." In the Season 6 episode "Blind Love," Nick and his friends are the target of a revenge plot that involves a potion called Amor Di Infierno, which, loosely translated, means "Love of Hell." Sounds lovely, right? It causes the drinker to fall madly in love with a specific person and, ultimately, become so overwhelmed with emotion that he or she self-destructs. This potion can only be created with the saliva (yum!) of a kind of Wesen called a Cupitas, along with a piece of hair from the target love interest and any liquid carrier. Cupitas saliva appears green, so to represent it, I made a concoction of Chartreuse, pear juice, honey, and bitters. We'll just go ahead and skip the pieces of hair …

SERVES 1

1 fl oz (30 ml) Chartreuse
1 fl oz (30 ml) pear juice
1 teaspoon Honey Syrup (page 14)
Dash of Angostura bitters
Ice cubes
3–4 fl oz (90–120 ml) brut
  Champagne

1 First, make the Cupidita's saliva (yum …). In a cocktail shaker, combine the Chartreuse, pear juice, syrup, and bitters with a few ice cubes. Shake well.

2 Strain into a champagne glass.

3 Top with Champagne.

GIGGLE WATER

INSPIRED BY **FANTASTIC BEASTS AND WHERE TO FIND THEM**

Fantastic Beasts is a prequel to the Harry Potter films but it is only loosely connected to the events of the original series. It takes place in the 1920s, as magical animal rights activist Newt Scamander visits the United States to return a magical creature to its natural habitat. "Giggle water" is actually an old-timey American term for Champagne, though you don't need to be a Legilimens to know this stuff ain't just Champagne! Using thoroughly American ingredients like bourbon and apple cider, this delicious shooter is as American as apple pie (kinda tastes like it, too), and it will make you burst out laughing.

SERVES 6

3 fl oz (90 ml) bourbon
1 fl oz (30 ml) butterscotch
  Schnapps
2 fl oz (60 ml) spiced apple cider
  (non alcoholic)
Ice cubes
3 fl oz (90 ml) Champagne

1 Add the bourbon, Schnapps, and cider to a mixing glass with a couple of ice cubes. Stir.

2 Divide among 6 shot glasses and top each shot with Champagne.

3 Drink in one gulp.

4 Laugh uncontrollably.

SUGGESTED SERVING VESSELS:

Shot glasses

CHATEAU ROMANI

INSPIRED BY **THE LEGEND OF ZELDA**

Majora's Mask is a game that has tons of strange and fascinating side quests. My two favorites are the ones that result in Link getting some booze-milk. Described as a "vintage" milk, a serving of the stuff fully restores Link's health and boosts his magic meter, making it the most useful consumable in the game. But drinking too much just makes you a sad drunk like Gorman. It is only produced by the very special cows at Romani Ranch. Preventing their abduction by aliens is the best way to get a free bottle, and since one bottle costs a whopping 200 rupees at the Milk Bar in Clock Town, you're definitely better off saving the cows. Put on your cow mask and savor this decadent vintage milk, which is enhanced with bourbon, Irish cream liqueur, and a hint of coffee liqueur to restore your energy.

SERVES 2

1 cup (235 ml) whole milk
2 fl oz (60 ml) bourbon
2 fl oz (60 ml) Irish cream liqueur
1 fl oz (30 ml) coffee liqueur
2 small scoops of vanilla ice cream
1 teaspoon vanilla extract
Pinch of ground cinnamon
Pinch of grated nutmeg

1 Blend all the ingredients in a blender.

2 Pour into one or 2 glass bottles.

SUGGESTED SERVING VESSEL:

Glass cork bottle

SUGGESTED EFFECT:

The Shimmer Effect (page 23)

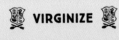 **VIRGINIZE**

Omit the bourbon, use non-alcoholic Irish cream, and replace the coffee liqueur with brewed coffee (30 ml) of brewed coffee.

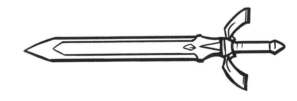

HERO DRINK

INSPIRED BY **FINAL FANTASY**

Final Fantasy is a series of science-fantasy RPGs developed by Square (now Squaresoft). The Hero Drink, also called "Hero Cocktail," is a recurring item in the *Final Fantasy* series, first appearing in *Final Fantasy V*. Although the effects vary from game to game, it's generally a powerful stat booster. The color, whenever depicted, is always a bright Chocobo yellow. Drink this to cause 9999 damage. To your liver.

SERVES 1–2

2 fl oz (60 ml) light rum
1 fl oz banana Schnapps
1–2 fl oz (30–60 ml) orange juice (without pulp)
2 fl oz (60 ml) pineapple juice
Ice cubes

1 Add all the ingredients to a cocktail shaker with some ice. Shake until cold, about 20 seconds.

2 Pour into a bottle to serve.

SUGGESTED SERVING VESSEL:

Small glass bottle

SUGGESTED EFFECT:

The Sparkly Rim (page 19) in yellow

 **VIRGINIZE**

Replace the rum with 2 fl oz (60 ml) white grape juice and a squeeze of fresh lemon juice. Replace the banana Schnapps with a couple drops of banana extract.

MIRUVOR

INSPIRED BY **THE LORD OF THE RINGS**

The Lord of the Rings by J.R.R. Tolkien is the quintessential high-fantasy series. One thing Tolkien is known for is his extensive world-building. Ever the craftsmen, the Elves of this series, make some great things: bread, swords, tree houses … One of the more memorable Elven gifts given to the fellowship was Miruvor. Also known as the nectar of the Valar, it was said to be made from Yavanna's flowers and thought to include honey. Clear in color, with warming properties, Miruvor helped the fellowship survive the journey through the treacherous Misty Mountains. Become "Lord of the Drinks" with this warm, floral, and invigorating beverage.

SERVES 1

3 fl oz (90 ml) white tea, lightly
  brewed and hot
1½ fl oz (45 ml) elderflower liqueur
1½ fl oz (45 ml) gin (Plymouth or
  London Dry)
2–3 teaspoons Honey Syrup
  (page 14), or to taste
1 teaspoon orange blossom water

1 Pour the tea into the serving vessel.

2 Stir in all the other ingredients.

SUGGESTED SERVING VESSELS:

Glass bottle
Crystal goblet

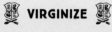

🛡 VIRGINIZE 🛡

Omit the gin, add another
1 fl oz (30 ml) of white
tea, and replace the
elderflower liqueur with
1 tablespoon (15 ml) of
either elderflower syrup or
Lavender Syrup (page 12).

RED POTION

Red potions have been a staple in video games for decades, appearing in popular titles like *The Legend of Zelda*, *World of Warcraft*, *Terraria*, and many, many more. Red-colored potions, more ubiquitously called "health potions" or "healing potions," usually restore a character's health or vitality, making them some of the most used and most common potions in many games. This recipe has some health benefits from the cranberry juice and ginger syrup. It seems counterintuitive to add alcohol to a health drink, but, hey, sometimes a little liquid courage doesn't hurt!

SERVES 1

1½ fl oz (45 ml) silver tequila
1 fl oz (30 ml) Campari
½ fl oz (15 ml) sweet vermouth
1 fl oz (30 ml) cran-raspberry juice
Ice cubes
2 fl oz (60 ml) soda water, chilled

1 Add all the ingredients except the soda water to a cocktail shaker with 2–3 ice cubes. Shake until chilled, about 20 seconds.

2 Pour the contents of the cocktail shaker into the bottle or other serving cup.

3 Top with the chilled soda water.

SUGGESTED SERVING VESSEL:

Glass bottle
Small cauldron

SUGGESTED EFFECTS/GARNISHES:

The Skewer (page 20) with strawberries cut into
    heart shapes
The Shimmer Effect (page 23, in red, gold, or silver)
The Mist Effect (page 24)

BLUE POTION

INSPIRED BY **YOUR FAVORITE VIDEO GAME**

Like red potions, blue potions are an RPG staple. Blue potions generally restore the player's magic points or "mana" (although occasionally it improves stamina or other stats). Since most of us don't have mana points to restore, I thought electrolytes and potassium might work. This cocktail has a nice tropical-citrus flavor, and with a bit of coconut water it will definitely refresh you … if not your mana.

SERVES 1

1 fl oz (30 ml) white rum
1 fl oz (30 ml) coconut rum
¾ fl oz (22 ml) blue curaçao
3 fl oz (30 ml) sparkling coconut
 water
2 tablespoons (30 ml) fresh
 lime juice
2 tablespoons (30 ml) Classic Simple
 Syrup (page 10), or to taste
2–3 ice cubes
2–3 fl oz (60–90 ml) lemon-lime
 soda

1 In a mixing glass, combine both rums, blue curaćao, coconut water, lime juice, simple syrup, and ice cubes. Stir.

2 Pour into a potion bottle or other serving glass.

3 Top with cold lemon-lime soda.

SUGGESTED SERVING VESSELS:

Potion bottle
Small cauldron

SUGGESTED EFFECTS:

The Shimmer Effect (page 23) in blue or silver
The Mist Effect (page 24)

GREEN POTION

In most games where they appear, the green potions restore stamina, although there are some outliers. The magic ingredient in this delicious potion is matcha green tea powder, which will restore all your stamina—all of it!—and give you a healthy dose of nutrients to boot.

SERVES 1

1 tablespoon (8 g) matcha powder
1 tablespoon (15 ml) warm water
1 fl oz (30 ml) vodka
1 fl oz (30 ml) Midori
2–3 ice cubes
1 scoop of lime sherbet
2–3 fl oz (60–90 ml) lemon-lime
  soda

1 Whisk the matcha powder with the water until the powder is completely dissolved.

2 In a cocktail shaker, add the vodka, Midori, matcha mix, and ice cubes. Shake until chilled and well combined.

3 Place the scoop of sherbet in the bottom of the bottle or other serving glass.

4 Pour the contents of the cocktail shaker on top of the lime sherbet.

5 Top with lemon-lime soda.

SUGGESTED SERVING VESSELS:

Glass bottle
Small cauldron

SUGGESTED EFFECTS:

The Shimmer Effect (see page 23)
The Mist Effect (page 24)

5
SCI-FI SPIRITS

Mass Effect: **RYNCOL COCKTAIL**

Firefly: **MUDDER'S MILK**

Firefly: **SHIMMERWINE**

Battlestar Galactica: **AMBROSIA**

Dune: **SPICE BEER**

Star Trek: **BLOODWINE**

Star Trek: **SAMARIAN SUNSET**

Star Trek: **ROMULAN ALE**

Star Wars: **ARDEES AKA JAWA JUICE**

Star Wars: **TATOOINE SUNSET**

The Hitchhiker's Guide to the Galaxy: **PAN GALACTIC GARGLE BLASTER**

RYNCOL COCKTAIL

INSPIRED BY **MASS EFFECT**

You spend a good amount of time in bars in BioWare's *Mass Effect 2* (at least, I did). In a game where you can get drunk and get private dances from aliens, why would you not do exactly that? Ryncol is a Krogan liquor, and anyone who has seen a Krogan knows that it's probably not a soft beverage. The pure form of Ryncol will kill a Volus and can put a human in a coma. In the game, if Shepherd orders five drinks at the Dark Star Lounge in the Citadel, the bartender will serve him/her a green Ryncol cocktail. If Shepherd drinks it, he/she will black out and wake up on the bathroom floor. Drink this and you may end up there yourself, possibly in a space bar in the twenty-second century.

SERVES 1

Ice cubes
1½ fl oz (45 ml) overproof white rum
1½ fl oz (45 ml) Midori
½ fl oz/1 tablespoon (15 ml)
    absinthe
1 tablespoon (15 ml) Classic Simple
    Syrup (page 10), or to taste
2–3 tablespoons (30–45 ml)
    fresh lime juice
Drop of mint extract
2–3 fl oz (60-90 ml) lemon-lime
    soda

1 Fill a cocktail shaker with ice.

2 Add all the ingredients, except the soda, to the cocktail shaker and shake well.

3 Strain the drink into a serving glass.

4 Top with lemon-lime soda.

SUGGESTED SERVING VESSEL:

Cocktail glass
Lowball glass

SUGGESTED GARNISH:

Sky blue rock candy
Sugar Rim (page 18) in sky blue

MUDDER'S MILK

INSPIRED BY FIREFLY

Someone recently told me that Browncoats need to let Joss Whedon's sci-fi series, *Firefly*, go. I said, "裝蛋." Mudder's Milk appeared in the episode "Jaynestown." It was created in Canton, a town on a planet called Higgin's Moon. Because mudding is such strenuous work, it was prudent for the laborers to get their nutritional requirements while they got their recreational drinking on. This mysterious concoction is supposed to have all the protein, vitamins, and carbs of a turkey dinner, plus 15% alcohol. Judging from Wash's reaction, the drink is definitely supposed to be an acquired taste, but I thought it would be a nice idea to make it more palatable.

SERVES 1-2

2 fl oz (60 ml) bourbon
2 fl oz (60 ml) Irish cream liqueur
1 cup (235 ml) whole milk
½ cup (125 g) plain Greek yogurt
1 frozen banana
2 tablespoons (30 g) peanut butter
¼ cup (20 g) oatmeal
1 tablespoon (12 g) flax seeds
1 tablespoon (10 g) chia seeds
2 teaspoons Spiced Maple Syrup
  (see page 15), or to taste
Pinch of ground cinnamon, or
  to taste
½ cup crushed ice

1 Combine all the ingredients in a blender.

2 Blend until smooth.

3 Pour into your serving vessel.

4 Sing an ode to Jayne, the hero of Canton!

SUGGESTED SERVING VESSEL:

Clay mug

VIRGINIZE

Omit the bourbon and use non-alcoholic Irish cream, or add more Spiced Maple Syrup (page 15).

BONUS DOUBLE-GEEK FUN FACT

Mudder's Milk is also a consumable in *World of Warcraft*. Shiny!

SHIMMERWINE

INSPIRED BY FIREFLY

Shimmerwine had a brief appearance in the episode "Shindig," and was sort of a throwaway line muttered by Inara when she was avoiding an uncomfortable conversation with Atherton Wing (aka "that piece of go-se"). Although it's not a huge part of the *Firefly* world—it *might* have been, *eventually*, but we'll never know because it was *cancelled*! Deep breaths, count to ten … the drink sounds pretty intriguing. I imagined a soft, shimmering effervescent beverage that, unlike Mal, would be right at home at fancy balls. Make it a mighty fine shindig and drink this (literally) shining cocktail while you question that buffet table.

SERVES 2

2 fl oz (60 ml) St Germain
  elderflower liqueur
1 fl oz (30 ml) vodka or gin
8 fl oz (240 ml) Champagne, chilled

1 Pour the St Germain and vodka or gin into 2 wine glasses or champagne flutes. Give it a quick stir.

2 Top off with the chilled Champagne.

SUGGESTED EFFECTS:

The Sparkly Rim (page 19) in gold or champagne
The Shimmer Effect (page 23) in gold

AMBROSIA

INSPIRED BY **BATTLESTAR GALACTICA**

Battlestar Galactica is a 1970s sci-fi series, created by Glen A. Larson, in which humanity is threatened by robotic antagonists called Cylons. The series was beautifully reimagined in 2004 by Ronald D. Moore and David Eick. In *BSG*, Ambrosia was an expensive, strong spirit that became rare after the twelve colonies were destroyed by the Cylons. Although Ambrosia is brown in the original series, it is bright green in the rebooted series, and this is the version I'm making. So, yes, I've already made a couple versions of the green Ambrosia[m]all of this has happened before, and all of this will happen again, am I right? This recipe (the best one, yet!) combines Navy Strength gin, melon liqueur, and citrus to make a very potent alcoholic beverage. As Gaeta says, "Ambrosia's good with a chaser." I suggest beer. Don't let the toasters get you down!

SERVES 1

2 fl oz (60 ml Navy Strength gin
1½ fl oz (45 ml) melon liqueur
½ oz (15 ml) Triple Sec
2 tablespoons (30 ml) fresh
   lime juice
1–3 dashes of angostura bitters
Ice cubes

1 Add all the liquid ingredients into a cocktail shaker filled with ice. Shake well.

2 Strain into a serving glass.

SUGGESTED SERVING VESSELS:
Cocktail glass
Champagne glass

SPICE BEER

INSPIRED BY DUNE

Frank Herbert's *Dune* is perhaps the most expansive sci-fi classic where everyone is addicted to drugs. In this world, the Spice Melange is a coveted but highly addictive substance that expands the awareness of the imbiber, which is necessary for interstellar travel. The taste and smell of this spice was described as similar to cinnamon, although more bitter. Melange can be mixed into both food and beverages as an enhancement, which is where Spice Beer comes in. This delicious beer cocktail combines the taste of cinnamon with lemon juice and spicy bitters. The spice beer must flow!

SERVES 1-2

1½ fl oz (45 ml) cinnamon liqueur
1½ fl oz (45 ml) bourbon
1 teaspoon fresh lemon juice
2–3 dashes Peychaud's Bitters
2–3 teaspoons Cinnamon Syrup
   (page 13), or to taste
3–4 fl oz (90–120 ml) IPA beer,
   chilled

1 In the serving glass(es), stir together the cinnamon liqueur, bourbon, lemon juice, bitters, and Syrup.

2 Top with beer and give it one last quick stir.

BLOODWINE

INSPIRED BY **STAR TREK**

———— ✦ ————

Klingons started as fairly one-dimensional antagonists in the original series and became more complex in *TNG* and *DS9*, when their culture and history were explored in depth. Bloodwine is a Klingon beverage that is so strong, non-Klingons can barely tolerate it. Although the taste of the beverage is never described, the appearance is blood red. The drink may or may not contain actual blood. In the official cookbook, Neelix states that it does, but Neelix isn't even from the Alpha quadrant, and, well, his expertise is dubious. It's more likely that it was named for its blood-like appearance, much like Sangria. tlhIngan maH'

SERVES 1

1½ fl oz (45 ml) dry sherry
1 fl oz (30 ml) overproof spiced rum
½ fl oz/1 tablespoon cherry liqueur
2–3 teaspoons (15–30 ml) Grenadine
  (page 11), or to taste
1–2 tablespoons (15–30 ml) fresh
  lemon juice
2–3 dashes of orange bitters
Ice cubes

1 Add all the ingredients to a cocktail shaker with a couple of ice cubes. Shake well.

2 Strain into the serving glass.

3 Qapla'.

SUGGESTED SERVING VESSELS:

Mug
Goblet

SAMARIAN SUNSET

INSPIRED BY STAR TREK

The Samarian Sunset is an intriguing beverage. The most interesting feature is that it starts out as clear liquid and then explodes with iridescent color when subjected to vibration (flicking the glass). The two most notable appearances are in *TNG* and *DS9*. Data makes one for Deanna Troi after losing their game of chess, as per their agreement. In *DS9*, Quark prepares the drink for his old flame, Natima Lang. The special effects of this drink are impossible to replicate exactly in the twenty-first century, but using the Sake Bomb technique comes pretty close!

SERVES 1

Ice cubes
2 fl oz (60 ml) coconut water
1 fl oz (30 ml) white rum
¾ fl oz (22 ml) shimmery white rum
 (see The Shimmer Effect, page 23)
½ fl oz (15 ml) pineapple juice
½ fl oz (15 ml) Grenadine (page 11)

1   Fill a cocktail shaker with ice and add the coconut water and 1 fl oz (30 ml) white rum. Shake well.

2   Strain into a highball glass.

3   In a separate double shot glass, add the shimmery white rum, pineapple juice, and grenadine.

4   Place two kabob skewers or chopsticks about a thumb's width distance apart across the top of the highball glass. Rest the shot glass on top.

5   Using your fists, slam the table until the shot falls between the skewers and into the glass, exploding with color and eventually settling into a uniform orange. (Alternatively, you can flick the glass fairly hard until the shot drops, but unless you're an android, this might take a few tries.)

SUGGESTED SERVING VESSELS:

Highball glass
Double shot glass

ROMULAN ALE

INSPIRED BY **STAR TREK**

Gene Roddenberry's *Star Trek* has a way of taking extremes of the human condition, sticking them in alien races, and forcing us to deal with them diplomatically. Romulans are obviously our snarky side. Their ale has been mentioned (or has appeared) in *TOS*, *TNG*, *DS9*, and some of the films. This highly intoxicating, bright blue stuff is so strong that even Klingons, who are resistant to most alcohols, suffer the aftermath. Romulan Ale has a strange legal status in the world of *Star Trek*, although if that's due to its strength or to the strained relations of the Federation with Romulans, Q only knows.

SERVES 1-2

2 fl oz (60 ml) overproof white rum
1 fl oz (30 ml) blue curaçao
1–2 tablespoons (15–30 ml) fresh
   lemon juice
Ice cubes
3 fl oz (90 ml) ginger beer, chilled

1   Add the rum, blue curaçao, and lemon juice to a cocktail shaker filled with ice.

2   Shake well.

3   Pour the contents of the shaker into a serving glass.

4   Top with ginger beer.

ARDEES AKA JAWA JUICE

INSPIRED BY STAR WARS

For a desolate desert planet, Tatooine produces a lot of good things: valuable ores, Bantha milk, Skywalkers ... Another fantastic Tatooine export is Jawa Juice, also known as "Ardees." I know the nickname *Jawa Juice* is somewhat alarming; the good news is that Ardees is made *by* Jawas, not *from* Jawas. The bad news is that it *is* made from mashed Bantha hides and fermented grains. The latter isn't so bad—fermented grains are the basis of many great things, like beer! However, Bantha hides are, well, perhaps not the most appetizing ingredient. If I had to imagine a taste, I would say they would taste smoky. This tasty draught combines two kinds of fermented grain alcohols, some citrus, Peychaud's bitters, and Spiced Maple Syrup, with a finish of bacon-infused ale for the ... uh ... protein.

SERVES 1

2 fl oz (60 ml) rye whiskey
3–4 teaspoons Spiced Maple Syrup
  (see page 15), or to taste
1 tablespoon (15 ml) fresh
  lemon juice
2–3 dashes of Peychaud's bitters
Ice cubes
3 fl oz (90 ml) bacon ale, chilled

1 Shake the whiskey, syrup, lemon juice, and bitters in a cocktail shaker with 2–3 ice cubes.

2 Pour into a serving glass.

3 Top with the chilled bacon ale.

SUGGESTED GARNISH:

Bacon salt

  VIRGINIZE

Use non-alcoholic spiced apple cider in place of the whiskey. Reduce the syrup quantity and use ginger ale and a dash of liquid smoke in place of the bacon ale.

TATOOINE SUNSET

INSPIRED BY **STAR WARS**

The *Star Wars* cantina is iconic—especially Chalmun's Cantina on Mos Eisley, that wretched hive of scum and villainy. You probably have the music in your head right now. It's understandable: This cantina is where you first saw some of the more colorful aliens that occupy that galaxy far, far away. It's where Obi-Wan unleashed the Force on that ruffian's arm. It's where Han shot first. In the movies, the drinks enjoyed at the cantina are mostly a mystery, but the companion materials, like *Star Wars: Absolutely Everything You Need to Know*, elaborates on them. Among the top five drinks served at Chalmun's is the Tatooine Sunset. This interpretation looks like a sunset with a bright Bantha blue top and uses spirits developed from desert plants like agave (tequila) and pomegranate.

SERVES 1

1½ fl oz (45 ml) silver tequila
½ fl oz (15 ml) blue curaçao
1 fl oz (30 ml) pomegranate liqueur
½ fl oz Grenadine (page 11)
　Cracked ice
1–2 tablespoons (15–30 ml) fresh
　lemon juice
2–3 fl oz (60–90 ml) orange juice
2 cherries

1 In a small mixing glass, stir together the tequila and blue curaçao. Set aside.

2 In the serving glass, add the pomegranate liqueur and grenadine. Then fill the glass with cracked ice.

3 Add the lemon juice and the orange juice to the serving glass.

4 Carefully pour the tequila and blue curaçao mixture over the back of a spoon so it slowly pours on top of the orange juice.

5 Garnish with the cherries and serve immediately!

SUGGESTED GARNISH:

Skewer (page 20) with 2 cherries (to represent both of Tatooine's suns)

 VIRGINIZE

Replace the blue curaçao with blue curaçao syrup. Replace the tequila with white grape juice. Replace the pomegranate liqueur with pomegranate juice.

PAN GALACTIC GARGLE BLASTER

INSPIRED BY THE HITCHHIKER'S GUIDE TO THE GALAXY

The Hitchhiker's Guide to the Galaxy, by Douglas Adams, is one of the most beloved sci-fi comedies of all time. As such, no fictional cocktail compendium would be complete without the most infamous cocktail in the universe: the Pan Galactic Gargle Blaster. Considered by the *Guide* to be the best drink in existence, the effects are described as, well … it involves the bludgeoning of one's brains with a lemon-wrapped gold brick. Never drink more than two, if you know where your towel is.

SERVES 1

1 sugar cube (Algolian Suntiger tooth)

2 dashes of lemon or grapefruit bitters (Zamphuor)

3 fl oz (90 ml) tonic water (Santragian seawater)

1 tablespoon (15 ml) fresh lemon juice

1 fl oz (30 ml) moonshine (Ol' Janx Spirit)

2 fl oz (60 ml) London dry gin (Arcturan Mega-gin)

Drop of crème de menthe (Qalactin Hypermint extract)

Small piece of dry ice (Fallian marsh gas)

1 Add the sugar cube to the cocktail glass.

2 Add the bitters and about 1 tablespoon (15 ml) of the tonic water.

3 Muddle the sugar cube to dissolve it.

4 Add the lemon juice, moonshine, gin, crème de menthe, and the remaining tonic water.

5 Stir the cocktail. Then, using the methods on page 25, add the dry ice.

SUGGESTED SERVING VESSEL:

Cocktail glass

SUGGESTED GARNISHES/EFFECTS:

Olive
The Mist Effect (page 24)

6
CULTY COCKTAILS

SONIC SCREWDRIVER

INSPIRED BY **DOCTOR WHO**

Okay, this one is not in the series canon, but the pun is just too good to pass up. The Doctor always carries a Sonic Screwdriver, a handy device with multiple uses that change to suit each of the Doctor's regenerations. In bartending, a "screwdriver" is vodka and orange juice, as many of you know. This version of a screwdriver uses blue curaçao, a blue, orange-flavored liqueur that makes the drink a nice Tardis blue.

SERVES 1

2 fl oz (60 ml) vodka
1 fl oz (30 ml) blue curaçao liqueur
2 teaspoons fresh lemon juice
1–3 teaspoons Classic Simple Syrup
  (page 10), or to taste
Ice cubes
3–4 fl oz (90–120 ml) orange-
  flavored sparkling water, or to
  taste

1 In your serving glass, stir together the vodka, Blue Curaćao, lemon juice, and simple syrup.

2 Add ice to the glass and top with the sparkling water.

SUGGESTED SERVING VESSEL:

Cocktail glass

SUGGESTED GARNISH:

The Sparkly Rim (page 19) in blue
Edible star sprinkles

EMERGENCY PROTOCOL 417

INSPIRED BY **DOCTOR WHO**

This drink appeared in Season 2 of the rebooted series, in "The Doctor Dances," an episode featuring gas masks, Moonlight Serenade, and a banana. Captain Jack Harkness—companion of the Ninth and Tenth Doctors, central character in the popular *Torchwood* spin-off, conman, and all-around fashionable guy—has to carry a bomb away from Earth that would destroy London. A couple of minutes from annihilation, he asks his computer to initiate "Emergency Protocol 417," which turns out to be a martini. A martini that's just a bit heavy on the vermouth. So, now you know what to do if you have only a few minutes left to live!

SERVES 1

Ice cubes
1½ fl oz (45 ml) gin, chilled
1½ fl oz (45 ml) dry vermouth
1 olive

1 Chill a coupe or martini glass in the fridge.

2 Add ice to a mixing glass, then pour in the gin and vermouth.

3 Stir for about half a minute.

4 Strain into your serving vessel.

5 Skewer the olive with a toothpick and add to the drink.

6 Reminisce about your former executioners.

SUGGESTED SERVING VESSELS:

Coupe
Martini glass

SUGGESTED GARNISH:

1 Spanish olive

WHITE RUSSIAN

INSPIRED BY **THE BIG LEBOWSKI**

The Coen brothers sure do have a knack for making cult films, but the one that resonated most in its time is probably the tale of The Dude. There are three things to know about The Dude: He bowls, he chills, and he drinks White Russians. This is a classic White Russian, just the way The Dude likes it. Don't worry, it'll really tie the room together.

SERVES 1 DUDE

Cracked ice
2 fl oz (60 ml) vodka
1½ fl oz (45 ml) coffee liqueur
1½ fl oz (45 ml) half-and-half

1 Add cracked ice to a rocks glass.

2 Pour in the vodka, followed by the coffee liqueur.

3 Top with half-and-half.

4 Stir.

SUGGESTED SERVING VESSEL:

Lowball/rocks glass

SUGGESTED DRINKING ATTIRE:

Bathrobe
Flip-flops

BLACK YUKON SUCKER PUNCH

INSPIRED BY **TWIN PEAKS**

This drink is almost as much of a mystery as *Twin Peaks* itself. Appearing in the episode "The Orchid's Curse," Judge Sternwood orders the beverage for Agent Cooper and Sheriff Truman while they discuss the trial of Leo Johnson. The drink appears to be black liquid topped with a light blue foam. The taste is not described, but Judge Sherwood tells Cooper and Truman that the drink will "sneak up on you." This interpretation features the two most important *Twin Peaks* food groups: black coffee and cherry. It's sweetened with Spiced Maple Syrup because nothing beats the taste sensation when maple syrup collides with ... spices. To complete the cocktail, create a couple of peaks in that mysterious blue foam. If Coop drank alcohol, he'd say, "That's a damn fine cup of booze!"

SERVES 1-2

1 fl oz (30 ml) bourbon
1 fl oz (30 ml) Yukon Jack or other
  honey liqueur
1 fl oz (30 ml) cherry liqueur
3 fl oz (90 ml) bold coffee, chilled
4 teaspoons Spiced Maple Syrup
  (page 15), or to taste
Ice cubes
5 egg whites
2 fl oz (60 ml) blue curaçao
½ tablespoon fresh lemon juice
1 teaspoon cream of tartar

1 Add the bourbon, liqueurs, coffee, and 2 teaspoons (10 ml) of syrup to a cocktail shaker, along with a few ice cubes. Shake well.

2 Strain into your serving vessel.

3 Add the egg whites, blue curaçao, lemon juice, cream of tartar, and the remaining 2 teaspoons (10 ml) of maple syrup to a mixing bowl and whip until (twin) peaks form.

4 Gently spoon the blue foam on top of the black liquid and smooth out the top of it.

SUGGESTED SERVING VESSEL:

Highball glass

TIP

The egg whites are "cooked" through the foaming process, but some folks may (understandably!) feel icky about using them. If you're one of those, skip steps 3 and 4 and do this instead:

1 cup (235 ml) heavy whipping cream
1 ½ fl oz (45 ml) blue curaçao

1 In a mixing bowl, whip the cream with the blue curaçao and the remaining 2 teaspoons of syrup.
2 Spoon the whipped cream mixture on top of the black liquid and smooth it out.

THREE-TOED SLOTH

INSPIRED BY COCKTAIL

It was hard to pick one of the crazy made-up drinks peppered in with the real-life cocktails in Tom Cruise's "Last Barman Poet" poem. There are many to choose from: The "Death Spasm"? The "Dingaling"? Honestly, I think we're all the scandalized lady in the audience incredulously asking, "Dingaling"?! But punning is my specialty, so I went with the Three-Toed Sloth. This cocktail uses sloe gin (get it?) with layers approximately the same colors as those of a three-toed sloth and topped with three coffee beans to act as the "toes."

SERVES 1

1 fl oz (30 ml) sloe gin
1 fl oz (30 ml) cognac
1 fl oz (30 ml) crème de cacao
1 fl oz (30 ml) Kahlúa
2 dashes of chocolate bitters
Ice cubes
1 fl oz (30 ml) heavy cream or
   coconut cream
3 coffee beans

1 In a cocktail shaker, combine the gin, cognac, crème de cacao, Kahlúa, bitters, and 2–3 ice cubes.

2 Pour the contents of the cocktail shaker into the serving glass.

3 Pour ⅓ of the heavy cream out of the carton and set aside (you can pour it back in later). Shake the heavy cream carton vigorously for about 30 seconds.

4 Hold a spoon upside down over the drink, pointed slightly downward. Slowly pour the cream onto the back of the spoon so that it indirectly spills over the rest of the drink, creating a separate layer. Top with the coffee beans.

SUGGESTED SERVING VESSEL:

Pousse-café glass

SUGGESTED GARNISH:

3 coffee beans

PURPLE NURPLE

INSPIRED BY **SUPERNATURAL**

Supernatural is a fantasy horror series, created by Eric Kripke, that follows brothers Sam and Dean Winchester as they hunt down dangerous supernatural creatures. Hunting is thirsty work, and although they do tend to drink mostly whiskey and beer, the brothers have been known to indulge in the occasional cocktail. Appearing in Season 2, "Tall Tales," Dean drinks this concoction while "interrogating" a local grad student at the campus bar. Presumably named Purple Nurple after the horrifying prank that involves twisting, well, you can guess … this purple shooter is surprisingly delicious. You really should try it.

SERVES 3-4

3 fl oz (90 ml) coconut rum
1 fl oz (30 ml) blue curaçao
1 fl oz (30 ml) Triple Sec
½ fl oz Grenadine (page 11),
  or to taste

1 In a mixing glass, stir together the rum, blue curaćao, Triple Sec, and Grenadine.

2 Pour the contents of the mixing glass into ¾ shot glasses.

SUGGESTED SERVING VESSEL:
  Shot glass

ORANGE WHIP

INSPIRED BY **THE BLUES BROTHERS**

The Blues Brothers is a 1980 American musical comedy based on a classic sketch from *Saturday Night Live*. One of the most quoted scenes in a movie filled with quotable material is the "Orange Whip" scene. Orange Whips were a brand of orange soda that served as the primary refreshment for the crew during filming. A crewmember, who had a relative working at the Orange Whip Corporation, asked the director if Orange Whip could be mentioned in the film. The famous scene was then completely improvised by John Candy.

This cocktail combines whipped cream vodka and orange soda for a cocktail that will make you see the light! There are 106 miles to Chicago …

SERVES 3

6 fl oz (175 ml) whipped cream
  vodka
1½ fl oz (45 ml) spiced rum
1½ fl oz (45 ml) Triple Sec
Ice cubes
9 fl oz (270 ml) orange soda

1 In a mixing glass, stir together the vodka, rum, Triple Sec, and 4–5 ice cubes.

2 Pour the contents of the mixing glass into 3 cocktail glasses.

3 Top each with 3 ounces (90 ml) of orange soda.

BLOOD

INSPIRED BY **YOUR FAVORITE VAMPIRE THING**

Ah, blood, the beverage of choice for vampires everywhere. I've said it before: Whether your favorite vampires are tortured souls, sparkly teenagers, ruthless killers, or werewolf-hating roommates in New Zealand, one thing they all have in common is their need for blood. Although there are some outliers in the vampire meta, blood generally has an addictive and intoxicating effect on vampires, much like alcohol has on mortals. This blood recipe contains cherries, along with two mortal vices—coffee and chocolate—to simulate what drinking blood might feel like to a vampire.

SERVES 1-2

3 fl oz (90 ml) tart cherry juice
½ cup (75 g) frozen pitted cherries
2 fl oz (60 ml) white rum
1 fl oz (30 ml) coffee liqueur
Dash of chocolate sauce
Dash of Grenadine (page 11)
Ice (optional)

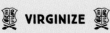 **VIRGINIZE**

Replace rum with
1 fl oz (30 ml) of water.
To replace the coffee
liqueur, mix 1 fl oz
(30 ml) of coffee with
1 oz (28 g) of sugar.

1 Add all the ingredients to a blender.

2 Blend on the lowest setting until smooth.

3 Let settle before serving.

SUGGESTED SERVING VESSEL:

Goblet

SUGGESTED EFFECTS:

The Candy Rim (page 19) in red
The Mist Effect (page 24)

VESPER

INSPIRED BY **JAMES BOND**

We all know the James Bond drink order, just like we all think it's really suave to say our last name, then our first name, then our last name again. It may surprise some of the film fans to learn that the shaken vodka martini wasn't always 007's signature drink. The original Bond novel *Casino Royale* (1953), written by Ian Fleming, mentions his first drink order as an Americano, a classic cocktail using equal parts Campari, sweet vermouth, and soda water. Bond's first martini order occurs later in the book. This special martini, called the Vesper after Bond girl Vesper Lynd, coincides with the birth of the "shaken, not stirred" catchphrase. The ingredients and ratios are given in the book, but since Kina Lillet is sadly discontinued, we have a modern substitution in this recipe.

SERVES 1

3 fl oz (90 ml) Gordon's gin
1 fl oz (30 ml) vodka
½ fl oz (15 ml) Lillet Blanc or Cocchi
   Americano
2–3 ice cubes

1 Put all the ingredients in a cocktail shaker and shake until ice cold, about 20 seconds.

2 Pour into your serving vessel.

SUGGESTED SERVING VESSEL:

   Deep champagne goblet

SUGGESTED GARNISH:

   The Spiral Citrus Peel (page 22) with lemon

BLACK FROST BEER

INSPIRED BY **BUFFY THE VAMPIRE SLAYER**

For some reason, "Beer Bad" seems to rate as one of the worst episodes of *Buffy the Vampire Slayer* in almost every ranking I've ever seen. I don't get it: Cave Buffy is the absolute best! In the episode, a bartender has been spiking Black Frost (one of the brews on tap at UC Sunnydale's campus pub) with a magic concoction that reverts drinkers into literal cavemen. The alchemic setup to make the beer is briefly shown. In it, acid is clearly labeled, but much of the bubbling mystery liquids seem to be distilled into a pale green serum that looks an awful lot like absinthe. Based on the name, I would guess Black Frost is a lager, because lager matures in cold storage. This is a refreshing, foamy beer cocktail that features absinthe, which will make most people act like Neanderthals in any case.

SERVES 1 THIRSTY SLAYER

1 fl oz (30 ml) absinthe
1–2 teaspoons Ginger Syrup
  (page 13), or to taste
2–3 dashes of grapefruit bitters
Squeeze of lime juice
3–4 fl oz (90–120 ml) light lager,
  chilled

1   Add the absinthe, syrup, bitters, and lime juice to a beer glass and stir.

2   Top off with a quick pour of the beer to make it more foamy, just how Cave-Buffy likes it.

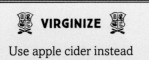 **VIRGINIZE**

Use apple cider instead
of beer. Omit the
absinthe or replace it
with anise syrup.

SINGAPORE SLING

INSPIRED BY **FEAR AND LOATHING IN LAS VEGAS**

The Singapore Sling is a classic cocktail, developed around 1915 by Ngiam Tong Boon, a bartender in Singapore. Perhaps the most notable reference to the drink is in Hunter S. Thompson's *Fear and Loathing in Las Vegas*. The main character, Duke, and his attorney are drinking Singapore Slings by the pool before receiving a catalytic call from Duke's editor. This is a fairly classic Singapore Sling, because, as Duke says, anything worth doing is worth doing right.

SERVES 1

Cracked ice and ice cubes
1½ fl oz (45 ml) gin
1 fl oz (30 ml) cherry brandy
½ fl oz/1 tablespoon (15 ml)
  Bénédictine
½ fl oz/1 tablespoon (15 ml)
  Triple Sec
3 fl oz (90 ml) pineapple juice
2 teaspoons Grenadine (page 11),
  or to taste
Squeeze of fresh lime juice
Dash of orange bitters

1 Fill a Collins glass with cracked ice.

2 Add all the liquid ingredients to a cocktail shaker with a couple of ice cubes. Shake well.

3 Strain the contents of the shaker into the serving vessel.

SUGGESTED SERVING VESSELS:

Hurricane glass
Collins glass

SUGGESTED GARNISHES:

Maraschino cherry
Pineapple slice
Cocktail umbrella
Sword skewer (page 20)

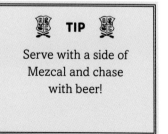

🛡 **TIP** 🛡
Serve with a side of
Mezcal and chase
with beer!

7
LITERARY
LIBATIONS

Harry Potter: **FIRE WHISKEY**

Harry Potter: **BUTTERBEER**

The Wheel of Time: **OOSQUAI**

Redwall: **STRAWBERRY CORDIAL**

Demon Cycle: **COUZI**

The Stormlight Archive: **VIOLET WINE**

A Song of Ice and Fire: **MULLED WINE**

Discworld: **SCUMBLE AND FLUFF**

FIREWHISKY

INSPIRED BY **HARRY POTTER**

Most fans think of the mildly alcoholic but still kid-friendly Butterbeer when they recall the magical beverages of the Harry Potter series, and with good reason: It sounds delicious and there's "butter" in the name! However, there's a more adult beverage to order at The Three Broomsticks. Firewhisky is referred to in four of the seven Harry Potter books, and Harry drinks it himself in *The Deathly Hallows* as a toast to Mad-Eye Moody. The taste is not described, but it burns Harry's throat and leaves him with a warm feeling like courage. It also seems to be a straight liquor, so I've created a simple whiskey cocktail with spicy cinnamon and orange notes.

SERVES 1

1 fl oz (30 ml) rye whiskey
½ fl oz/1 tablespoon (15 ml)
  Triple Sec
1½ fl oz (45 ml) cinnamon whiskey
1–2 teaspoons Cinnamon Syrup
  (page 13)
1–2 dashes of orange bitters
Ice cubes (optional)

1 In a mixing glass, stir together the rye whiskey, Triple Sec, cinnamon whiskey, syrup, and bitters.

2 Pour the mixture into the serving glass, which can have a few ice cubes in it or not, according to your preference. Enjoy!

SUGGESTED SERVING VESSELS:

Glencairn
Lowball glass

SUGGESTED EFFECT:

The Citrus Flame (page 29) with orange

BUTTERBEER

INSPIRED BY **HARRY POTTER**

The *Harry Potter* series by JK Rowling is the best-selling fantasy series of all time, so it comes as no surprise that Butterbeer is one of fiction's most renowned alcoholic beverages. You can actually get an official version at The Wizarding World of Harry Potter, at Universal Studios, but if you're like me, you'll want to enjoy it between visits. The alcoholic content of Butterbeer is supposed to be negligible—only containing enough alcohol to get a house elf drunk—so presumably an adult human would have to drink an awful lot of it to get any sort of buzz. Or an adult human could just spike it with some rum!

SERVES 3-4

3 cups (750 ml) stout beer
2 cinnamon sticks
8 whole cloves
8 whole allspice
1 tablespoon (14 g) imitation butter
1 tablespoon (14 g) butter melted
1 tablespoon (15 ml) vanilla extract
¼ cup (60 g) brown sugar
2 fl oz (60 ml) evaporated milk
1 fl oz (30 ml) sweetened condensed
  milk, (or to taste)
3–4 fl oz (90–120 ml) spiced rum

1 Pour the beer into a saucepan, along with the cinnamon sticks, cloves, and allspice.

2 Bring to a boil over a high heat, then lower the heat to medium-low and simmer for about 15 minutes.

3 Remove the spices (with a strained or slotted spoon), but keep the cinnamon sticks for serving.

4 Stir in the remaining ingredients and simmer for another couple of minutes.

5 Pour into 3–4 serving vessels.

SUGGESTED SERVING VESSEL:
Mug

SUGGESTED GARNISHES:
Cinnamon sticks
Whipped cream
Gold sprinkles

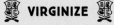 **VIRGINIZE**

Omit the rum and
use a dark
non-alcoholic beer.

OOSQUAI

INSPIRED BY **THE WHEEL OF TIME**

The Wheel of Time, written by Robert Jordan, is an expansive series of high-fantasy novels that have earned their elevated ranking among other fantasy best sellers. Oosquai is a potent drink of the Aiel, a desert-dwelling warrior race. Made from "zemai," which is the Aiel word for "corn," it is described as brown in color and stronger than double-distilled brandy. Conveniently for us, bourbon is also brown and made with mostly corn. Oosquai does seem to be a straight liquor, so here is a simple bourbon cocktail. Sharing Oosquai with someone is supposed to be a great act of friendship between warriors, so this recipe serves two: you and a friend. Dovie'andi se tovya sagain!

SERVES 2

4 fl oz (120 ml) bourbon
1 fl oz (30 ml) sweet vermouth
5–6 dashes of Angostura bitters
3–4 ice cubes

1   Fill the mixing glass with all the liquid ingredients, add ice, and stir gently for 10–15 seconds.

2   Strain into your serving vessel.

SUGGESTED EFFECTS/GARNISHES:

The Citrus Flame (page 29) with orange
The Spiral Citrus Peel (page 22) with orange

STRAWBERRY CORDIAL

INSPIRED BY **REDWALL**

Redwall is a beloved series of children's fantasy novels written by Brian Jacques. The books are chock-full of mouthwatering food and drink, so it's no wonder the series has its very own official cookbook written by Jacques himself. Strawberry Cordial, also called "Strawberry Fizz," is mentioned in almost every book and enjoyed at almost every celebration or feast. It's mainly described as bubbly, cold, and sweet. A cordial can be alcoholic or not; considering this cordial's popularity with the Dibbuns, it may not be alcoholic or it might be only slightly alcoholic. For our purposes, we'll booze it up a bit.

SERVES 2-4

¾ cup (150 g) granulated sugar
1½ cups (350 ml) water
2 pints (714 g) ripe strawberries
4 fl oz (120 ml) white rum
1 bottle (750 ml) prosecco, chilled

 **VIRGINIZE**

Omit the rum, increase the sugar to 1 cup (200 g), and replace the prosecco with seltzer water.

1 In a medium saucepan, heat the sugar, water, and strawberries over a medium heat until the liquid comes to a boil, stirring occasionally.

2 Once boiling, reduce to a simmer and continue to simmer for 20 minutes, or until the strawberries are tender.

3 Remove the strawberry mixture from the heat and transfer to a blender. Blend until smooth.

4 Place a fine-mesh strainer over a large pitcher and pour the mixture through it. Discard what's in the strainer (or use it for something else).

5 Add your rum to the pitcher, followed by the prosecco. Give it a gentle stir until just blended before pouring into serving glasses.

SUGGESTED SERVING VESSEL:

Cordial glass

SUGGESTED GARNISHES:

Fresh strawberry slices
Ice with strawberry slices (page 21)

COUZI

Demon Cycle, a fantasy-horror series by Peter V. Brett, takes place in a world where demons come every night to terrorize and kill humans. In this world, Couzi is an extremely potent drink made with fermented grains and cinnamon. Because of its potency, it is served in small cups, and its strong cinnamon smell burns the nostrils. Couzi and other grain alcohols are forbidden by the Evejah, a religious text in the world of *Demon Cycle*. I'm not sure which is scarier, the Evejah or the demon attacks. Seriously, how else are you supposed to cope with demon attacks???

SERVES 4

3 fl oz (90 ml) strong rye whiskey
1 fl oz (30 ml) cinnamon liqueur
3–4 teaspoons (15–20 ml) Cinnamon
   Syrup (page 13), or to taste
5–6 dashes of ground cinnamon
   or Peychaud's bitters
2–3 teaspoons (10–15 ml) fresh
   lemon juice
Ice cubes

1 Add all the liquid ingredients to a mixing glass with a few ice cubes and stir.

2 Pour into your serving vessels.

SUGGESTED SERVING VESSELS:

Shot glasses

VIOLET WINE

INSPIRED BY **THE STORMLIGHT ARCHIVE**

The Stormlight Archive, an epic fantasy series written by Brandon Sanderson (the author who completed *The Wheel of Time* series after Robert Jordan passed), takes place in a world that is periodically ravaged by violent storms. More importantly, the wines come in multiple colors! Violet wine is the most flavorful and intoxicating of the wines, which also include sapphire, orange, and yellow. This recipe combines rosé with crème de violette for a nice, deep purple wine that will definitely intoxicate you.

SERVES 1

1 fl oz (30 ml) crème de violette
½ fl oz (15 ml) raspberry liqueur
1 tablespoon (15 ml) lemon juice
2–3 ice cubes
4 fl oz (120 ml) dry rosé wine

1   Add the liqueurs and juice to a cocktail shaker with the ice cubes.

2   Strain into the serving vessel.

3   Top with the rosé and stir.

SUGGESTED EFFECT:

The Shimmer Effect (page 23)

MULLED WINE

The *A Song of Ice and Fire* novels and TV adaption *Game of Thrones* have become a phenomenon that's unprecedented for a fantasy series. Mulled wine appears throughout the series many times, as its warmth makes it a favorite of the men of the Night's Watch. Of course, mulled wine is a real thing that is omnipresent in fantasy literature; it's in everything from *The Canterbury Tales* to *The Elder Scrolls*. Originally called Hipprocras, this drink is at least as old as Rome. There are many versions of this delicious rich and spicy beverage across many cultures, both presently and historically, so this recipe is appropriate for any occasion, whether that's a nameday celebration, a (red, purple, or pink) wedding, or just your standard holiday party.

SERVES 8-10

1 orange
1 lemon
2 bottles (750 ml each) red wine
4–6 fl oz (120–175 ml) brandy
    (optional)
2-inch (5 cm) piece of fresh ginger,
    peeled and thinly sliced
5 cinnamon sticks
5 cloves
2 black peppercorns
5 whole nutmegs, to taste
8 whole allspice, to taste
¾ cup (255 g) honey, or to taste

1　Remove the zest from the orange and lemon in strips, using a knife or vegetable peeler. Set aside.

2　Juice the orange and lemon into a Dutch oven or thick-bottomed pot. Then pour the wine and brandy (if using) into the pot.

3　Add the orange and lemon zest, ginger, cinnamon sticks, cloves, peppercorns, nutmeg, allspice, and honey into the same pot and stir for a minute or two.

4　Cover the pot and heat over medium heat until the liquid is hot, being careful not to let it boil. Then reduce the heat to low and simmer for an hour, or until the spices are strong enough for your tastes.

5　Strain out the spices or remove them with a slotted spoon before serving.

SUGGESTED GARNISHES:
Whole spices
Citrus peels

SCUMBLE AND FLUFF

INSPIRED BY **DISCWORLD**

Discworld: everyone's favorite world resting upon the shoulders of four giant elephants standing upon a giant turtle that is floating through space. This is the setting of a beloved series of comedic fantasy novels written by the late and great Terry Pratchett. In *Discworld*, Scumble is made from apples and is strong enough to clean silverware, so it's served in very small amounts. When combined with dwarven ale, it creates a cocktail called "Fluff." Sometimes, you just need to imbibe vast amounts of alcohol.

SERVES 1-2

Ice cube
1 fl oz (30 ml) applejack brandy
3–4 dashes of apple bitters
1–3 teaspoons Spiced Maple Syrup
  (page 15), or to taste
½ fl oz (15 ml) Apple Pie Moonshine
  (optional)
4 oz (120 ml) bitter ale (optional,
  for Fluff)

1 Add ice to a mixing glass.

2 Pour in the brandy, bitters, syrup, and moonshine (if using). Stir.

3 Pour into your serving vessel(s).

4 Make it "fluff" by adding the ale.

SUGGESTED SERVING VESSELS:

Thimbles
Shot glasses

8
DYSTOPIAN POTIONS

VICTORY GIN

INSPIRED BY 1984

George Orwell's classic 1949 novel *Nineteen Eighty-Four* was doing dystopia way before it was cool. It takes place in Oceania, a terrifying version of England where residents are living under an oppressive political regime that watches their every move, and Victory is the only available brand of cigarettes and alcohol. Unsurprisingly, the taste of Victory gin is about as good as you would imagine oppressive government-issued liquor would be. According to Winston, the main character, it smells sickly sweet, like rice wine, and burns like nitric acid. Ah, the taste of conformity … . Remember, proles: Big Brother is watching you drink.

SERVES 1

1 fl oz (30 ml) dry gin
Dash of dry vermouth
Dash of mirin
Squeeze of fresh lemon juice
Dash of Angostura bitters
Ice cubes

1 Add all the liquid ingredients to a cocktail shaker with 2–3 ice cubes. Shake well.

2 Pour into a serving glass.

MOLOKO PLUS

INSPIRED BY **A CLOCKWORK ORANGE**

A Clockwork Orange is a 1962 dystopian novel by Anthony Burgess featuring a subculture of extremely violent youth gangs in near-future England. The disturbing film adaptation by Stanley Kubrick brought the story to the mainstream. Moloko Plus, also known as Knifey Moloko or Milk-Plus, was a special milk sold to minors at bars. Yes, Moloko Plus is laced with drugs. If you want to make a drug milkshake to peet while resting your nogas on your nagoy dama coffee table with your droogs, that's totally horrorshow. However, I propose that you make this instead. Drink while listening to some Ludwig Van; it'll make you have a warm vibratey feeling all through your guttiwuts.

SERVES 1-2

3 fl oz (90 ml) orange juice (freshly squeezed or unpasteurized)
2 fl oz (60 ml) half-and-half
1 fl oz (30 ml) vanilla vodka
1 fl oz (30 ml) white rum
½ fl oz/1 tablespoon (15 ml) Triple Sec
1 cup (140 g) crushed ice

1 Blend all the liquid ingredients in a blender with a cup or so of crushed ice.

2 Pour into serving glasses.

SUGGESTED GARNISHES:

The Spiral Citrus Peel (page 22) with orange
Orange slice

ATOMIC COCKTAIL

INSPIRED BY **FALLOUT**

Fallout, a dystopian game series developed by Bethesda Studios, takes place in an alternative retro-futuristic USA after a devastating nuclear war. The "Atomic Cocktail" appears in *Fallout: New Vegas*, one of the most beloved games in the series. You craft this drink using Nuka Cola Victory, vodka, and Mentats, which are red, highly addictive stimulants whose name is a reference to the Mentats of *Dune*, with their superhuman awareness and very red lips. Nuka Cola Victory radiates a unique orangey color, but the flavor is a mystery. My interpretation features Red Bull (for both its stimulating effect and its color), pineapple soda, and a vodka bomb shot.

SERVES 1

2 fl oz (60 ml) pineapple soda,
  chilled
1 fl oz (30 ml) Red Bull, chilled
2–3 teaspoons (10–15 ml) Grenadine
  (page 11), or to taste
2 tablespoons (30 ml) fresh
  lime juice
2 fl oz (60 ml) vodka

1 Add the soda and Red Bull to the serving glass. Give it a quick stir.

2 Stir in the grenadine and lime juice.

3 Pour the vodka into a shot glass, then drop it into the cola mixture and drink. Kaboom!

SUGGESTED SERVING VESSEL:

Highball glass

SUGGESTED EFFECT:

The Mist Effect (page 24)

NUKA COLA DARK

INSPIRED BY FALLOUT

The Nuka-World DLC is the sixth and final add-on to *Fallout 4*, essentially serving as the game's ending. In it, you explore the now-defunct Nuka-World, a theme park owned by the Nuka-Cola company. Many new flavors of sodas are introduced, from Nuka-berry to Nuka-cide, but we're focusing on the boozy one. Nuka-Cola Dark is an alcoholic version of Nuka-Cola, darker in color and containing a whopping 35% alcohol. The loading screen hints for Nuka-World tell you that the drink was touted as "the most refreshing way to unwind."

SERVES 1-2

Ice cubes
1 fl oz (30 ml) black vodka
1 fl oz (30 ml) spiced rum
1 fl oz (30 ml) raspberry liqueur
4–5 dashes of chocolate bitters
3–4 fl oz (60–90 ml) cola

1 Fill a mixing glass with ice cubes.

2 Add the vodka, rum, raspberry liqueur, and bitters. Stir.

3 Strain into your serving vessel(s) and top with cola.

SUGGESTED SERVING VESSEL:

Glass soda bottle

CAUTION

Do not operate motor vehicles or heavy machinery for at least 8 hours after drinking.

SOULSTORM BREW

Oddworld, created by developer Oddworld Inhabitants Inc., is a series of games that take place in a fictional world that has been ravaged by industrialization. SoulStorm Brew is a highly addictive drink made by the Glukkons, a greedy race of creatures who have enslaved many of the other races and are forcing them to work in their factories. Indeed, SoulStorm Brew is how they keep the other creatures, especially the Mudokons, under their thumb. As Abe, the main character, discovers, SoulStorm Brew is made from Mudokon bones and tears. This tart, sweet cocktail is unnaturally green and uses gelatin for the Mudokon bones and sea salt for the tears. If you drink too much, seek out the Three Weirdos!

SERVES 1-2

½ tablespoon lime Jell-O mix
¼ cup (60 ml) hot water
Ice cubes
2½ fl oz (75 ml) light rum
½ fl oz/1 tablespoon (15 ml) melon liqueur
Pinch of sea salt
2 fl oz (60 ml) lemon-lime soda

1 In a bowl, dissolve the gelatin in the hot water, stirring for a couple of minutes.

2 Add a few ice cubes, along with the rum, melon liqueur, and sea salt.

3 Pour into the serving glasses and top with lemon-lime soda.

9
COMEDIC CONCOCTIONS

Archer: **PEPPERMINT PATTY**

Archer: **6 GUMMY BEARS AND SOME SCOTCH**

Bob's Burgers: **SWANKY-PANKY**

Brooklyn Nine-Nine: **MOSS WINE**

The Simpsons: **FLANDERS' PLANTER'S PUNCH**

It's Always Sunny in Philadelphia: **FIGHT MILK**

The Nutty Professor: **ALASKAN POLAR BEAR HEATER**

Red Dwarf: **BEER MILKSHAKE**

PEPPERMINT PATTY

INSPIRED BY **ARCHER**

Archer is an adult animated sitcom created by Adam Reed that follows Sterling Archer, a promiscuous, egotistical secret agent, and his dysfunctional colleagues. We all wish we had Archer's talent for having a drink for every occasion, whether that occasion is a skiing trip, a totally ninja-assassination-extrajudicial killing, or both. In the Season 6 episode, "The Archer Sanction," as Archer, Lana, and Ray are driving to their target in the Alps, Archer pulls out his Thermos and gushes about how delicious his creamy concoction is, repeatedly asking Lana to try it. (LANA!!!) Following Archer's recipe pretty much verbatim, this tasty beverage will keep you warm in the Danger Zone!

SERVES 3-4

2 cups (470 ml) hot cocoa
1 teaspoon vanilla extract
¼ cup (60 ml) half-and-half
3½ fl oz (105 ml) dark crème
   de cacao
1 fl oz (30 ml) creme de mènthe
3½ fl oz (105 ml) peppermint
   Schnapps

1   Prepare the hot cocoa in a saucepan over medium heat and bring to a simmer.

2   Remove from the heat and add the vanilla, half-and-half, crème de cacao, crème de menthe, and peppermint Schnapps.

3   Pour into your serving vessel.

SUGGESTED SERVING VESSELS:

Thermos
Mugs

SUGGESTED GARNISHES:

Whipped cream
Cinnamon sticks
Candy canes

6 GUMMY BEARS AND SOME SCOTCH

INSPIRED BY **ARCHER**

Archer can make a cocktail out of pretty much anything, right? He's like the MacGyver of cocktails. I'm not sure I can really call this one a cocktail, but by god, I'm going to try. This is a reference to the first-season episode "Killing Utne," in which all Archer ate was six gummy bears and some Scotch. Oh, and Malory hatches a dinner party assassination scheme that goes awry, but what else is new?

SERVES 2

12 Haribo gummy bears
4 fl oz (120 ml) Scotch whisky, plus more for soaking

 TIP

Make sure you cover the Scotch and gummy bears while soaking, unless you want ants. Because that's how you get ants.

1   Add the gummy bears to a glass or small bowl. Pour in just enough Scotch whisky to cover them. Let them soak for at least 15 hours or overnight.

2   The gummy bears should be big and squishy now, having soaked up all or most of the alcohol. If there's a little alcohol left, that's fine—you can add it to the drink, or you can continue the soak until it's completely absorbed.

3   Split the gummies between 2 glasses. Pour 2 fl oz (60 ml) of the Scotch into each glass. Enjoy the delicious taste of Scotch with the occasional sweet, chewy gummy bear.

SWANKY-PANKY

INSPIRED BY **BOB'S BURGERS**

I know it's weird to do a *Bob's Burgers* recipe that isn't a burger, but someone else did the burger thing and did it really well. In the episode "Crawl Space," Teddy mentions that his family invented a cocktail called the "Swanky-Panky." Teddy manages to say the drink is two parts vermouth before Bob cuts him off. I wanted to know more, Bob! There is a classic cocktail called the Hanky-Panky, which may have been the inspiration. This recipe is a modified version of that, using Peychaud's bitters as a nod to the Sazerac, the favorite cocktail of *Bob's Burgers* creator Loren Bouchard. This may get you even more buzzed than Margarita Mix!

SERVES 1

Ice cube
2 fl oz (60 ml) sweet vermouth
1 fl oz (30 ml) dry gin
2 dashes of Peychaud's bitters
Orange peel

1   Add an ice cube to a mixing glass.

2   Add the vermouth, gin, and bitters to the mixing glass and stir until chilled.

3   Strain the contents of the mixing glass into a chilled coupe or martini glass.

4   Twist an orange peel over the surface of the drink to release the oil or use the Citrus Flame method on page 29.

5   Use the peel for garnish.

SUGGESTED SERVING VESSEL:

Coupe
Martini glass

SUGGESTED EFFECTS/GARNISHES:

The Citrus Flame (page 29) with orange
The Spiral Citrus Peel (page 22) with orange
Edible gold leaf flakes

MOSS WINE

INSPIRED BY **BROOKLYN NINE-NINE**

We're getting pretty meta over here, folks: This recipe is from a fake fantasy series within a police sitcom. *Brooklyn Nine-Nine*, created by Dan Goor and Michael Schur, revolves around Brooklyn's 99th Precinct. In the episode "Return to Skyfire," officers Peralta and Terry are investigating a claim by DC Parlov, writer of *The Skyfire Cycle*, a series of fantasy books of which Peralta and Terry are both fans. So, the two fanboys drag Rosa along as they go "undercover" at a fantasy convention. While they're there, they see a booth serving "Moss Wine," a drink mentioned in the *Skyfire* series. Terry wonders aloud if it's as gross as the books say it is. Well, Terry, it's not as gross as the books say it is … (title of your sex tape!).

SERVES 1

8–10 basil leaves
1 tablespoon (15 ml) fresh
  lemon juice
3 fl oz (90 ml) dry white wine
½ fl oz/1 tablespoon (15 ml)
  vermouth
1½ fl oz (45 ml) Ginger Syrup
  (page 13), or to taste
Ice cubes

1 In a cocktail shaker, muddle the basil with the lemon juice.

2 Add the remaining ingredients, plus an ice cube or two. Shake well.

3 Strain into a wine glass.

SUGGESTED SERVING VESSEL:
   Wine glass
   Goblet

SUGGESTED EFFECTS:
   The Mist Effect (page 24)
   The Candy Rim (page 19) in swampy green

FLANDERS' PLANTER'S PUNCH

INSPIRED BY **THE SIMPSONS**

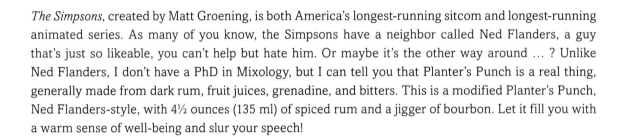

The Simpsons, created by Matt Groening, is both America's longest-running sitcom and longest-running animated series. As many of you know, the Simpsons have a neighbor called Ned Flanders, a guy that's just so likeable, you can't help but hate him. Or maybe it's the other way around … ? Unlike Ned Flanders, I don't have a PhD in Mixology, but I can tell you that Planter's Punch is a real thing, generally made from dark rum, fruit juices, grenadine, and bitters. This is a modified Planter's Punch, Ned Flanders-style, with 4½ ounces (135 ml) of spiced rum and a jigger of bourbon. Let it fill you with a warm sense of well-being and slur your speech!

SERVES 2-3

4½ fl oz (135 ml) spiced rum
1½ fl oz (45 ml) bourbon
½ fl oz/1 tablespoon crème
   de cassis
4 fl oz (120 ml) pineapple juice
3 fl oz (90 ml) orange juice
1 fl oz (30 ml) cold water
1 tablespoon (15 ml) lime juice
1 tablespoon Grenadine (page 11), or
   to taste
2 dashes of Angostura bitters
Ice cubes

1   Add all the liquid ingredients to a large mixing glass with 2–3 ice cubes and stir until well combined.

2   Open-pour into serving glasses. Add more ice if desired.

SUGGESTED SERVING VESSEL:

Clear plastic cup

SUGGESTED GARNISH:

Cherry

FIGHT MILK

INSPIRED BY IT'S ALWAYS SUNNY IN PHILADELPHIA

It's Always Sunny in Philadelphia is a black comedy following a group of five degenerates who run a Philadelphia pub, among other ill-conceived ventures. Fight Milk, in all its avian glory, appeared in the Season 8 episode "Frank's Back in Business." Charlie, with Mac's help, comes up with the perfect product for Atwater Company to sell: Fight Milk! Marketed as "the first alcoholic dairy-based protein drink for bodyguards, by bodyguards" in the promotional video, the ingredients include milk, vodka, and crow eggs. This version of the unusual beverage combines egg-based protein powder, vanilla vodka, and malted milk to make something not only edible but actually pretty tasty. Fight like a crow! :: **crow sounds** ::

SERVES 1-2

2½ fl oz (75 ml) vanilla vodka
1 cup (250 ml) whole milk
1 tablespoon egg protein powder
3 tablespoons malted milk powder
2–3 teaspoons (10–15 ml) Brown
  Sugar Syrup (page 14), or to taste
½ cup (70 g) crushed or cracked ice

1   Add all the ingredients to a blender and blend on high until smooth.

2   Pour into a serving glass.

3   Soar high as a crow!

SUGGESTED SERVING VESSEL:

Old plastic sports drink bottle

ALASKAN POLAR BEAR HEATER

INSPIRED BY **THE NUTTY PROFESSOR**

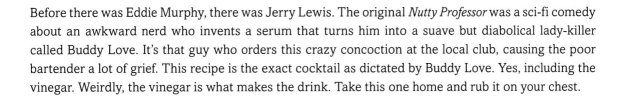

Before there was Eddie Murphy, there was Jerry Lewis. The original *Nutty Professor* was a sci-fi comedy about an awkward nerd who invents a serum that turns him into a suave but diabolical lady-killer called Buddy Love. It's that guy who orders this crazy concoction at the local club, causing the poor bartender a lot of grief. This recipe is the exact cocktail as dictated by Buddy Love. Yes, including the vinegar. Weirdly, the vinegar is what makes the drink. Take this one home and rub it on your chest.

SERVES 1-2

2 fl oz (60 ml) vodka
1 teaspoon rum
2 dashes of orange bitters
1 teaspoon apple cider vinegar
1 fl oz (30 ml) vermouth
1 fl oz (30 ml) gin
1 teaspoon brandy
1 teaspoon Scotch
Ice cubes

1 Pour all the ingredients into a cocktail shaker.

2 Shake it up "real nice."

3 Pour it into a tall glass.

4 Drink, and promptly pass out.

SUGGESTED GARNISHES:

The Spiral Citrus Peel with (page 22) lemon
The Spiral Citrus Peel with (page 22) orange
Maraschino cherry

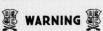 **WARNING**

You might actually turn to stone drinking this. Adding fresh lemon juice and Classic Simple Syrup (page 10) will make that less likely, however.

BONUS DOUBLE-GEEK FUN FACT

This concoction was also referenced in the delightfully cheesy 1980s space rom-com musical *Earth Girls Are Easy.*

BEER MILKSHAKE

INSPIRED BY RED DWARF

Beer is obviously the best milkshake flavor, right? Created by Rob Grant and Doug Naylor, *Red Dwarf* is a British sci-fi comedy TV series that aired from 1988 to 1999, and as of 2017 it has been rebooted as *Red Dwarf XII*. In the original series, Dave Lister is the last living human aboard a mining ship, along with an assortment of unusual companions. He invents the beer milkshake in the episode "Waiting for God" when ordering breakfast from the computer. After requesting chicken vindaloo and a milkshake, the computer asks him what flavor of milkshake he would like, to which he replies, "Erm, beer." Of course, Leopard Lager would be the best beer to use with this, but because it's in limited supply hereabouts, chocolate stout does a fine job pairing with chocolate ice cream. Enjoy with some spicy curry or chicken marengo!

SERVES 2-4

I pint/2 cups (475 ml) chocolate stout
2 fl oz (60 ml) crème de cacao
1 pint (475 g) chocolate ice cream
2 tablespoons (30 ml) chocolate
  sauce, or to taste, plus more
  for garnish

1 Pour the stout, crème de cacao, ice cream, and chocolate sauce into a blender and blend on low until just mixed, about 30 seconds. Be careful not to over-blend.

2 Drizzle chocolate sauce along the sides of 2–4 large glasses, and then pour the ice cream mixture into them.

SUGGESTED SERVING VESSEL:

Milkshake glass

SUGGESTED GARNISH:

Whipped cream with a maraschino cherry
Chocolate sauce

INDEX

ACKNOWLEDGMENTS

Tobias, my little Wolverine, thank you for sharing my energy and attention with this project. Jeff, thank you for picking up my slack. You are the best baby-daddy a geek could hope for.

Rolanda and Joe Conversino, thank you so much for helping me with the beastly Sucker Punch, and for everything else you do for my little family. A basket of kisses!

Kyle Cyree, words can't say how much I appreciate you lending me your time, grammar skills, mixology experience, and sick puns.

Denis Caron, as always, thank you taking the time to create the amazing illustrations for these bad boys.

Nicholas Reeder, I love you, big brother. Thank you for testing SO many recipes and spending so much on liquor. I hope you're putting the leftovers to good use. Francisco, thank you for tolerating blue curaçao on my account, jajaja!

Ashley Finley, my favorite cousin, and husband Zach, thank you so much for taking on so many recipes this time! Especially for making homemade (organic!) lavender syrup. I love you guys!

Allison Moore, my favorite cousin, and husband Danny, thank you for testing out all those drinks. You even took on the Alaskan Polar Bear Heater, and I cannot thank you enough for that. I love you guys!

Special thanks to Jay Perez, Miguel Martinez, and Lauren Rassel for testing (testing) out recipes—especially Lauren for taking the time to bestow her bartending wisdom and creativity upon me.

Amanda, Brian, and Beowulf Backur, thank you so much for drink testing, as always! Can't wait to see baby Kylo! I hope you have a lightsaber on your registry!

Jessica and Wes Garcia, you both have helped me so much with past books, I just wanted to make sure you were in this one, too.

Amanda J. Alvarez, I know you didn't get around to testing, but I very much appreciated you volunteering. I miss working with you and your sister and her sister from another mister.

Thanks to Jeannine Dillon for finding me in the first place, for continuing to give me these opportunities, and for your patience with me. Seriously, I cannot thank you enough.

Thanks to Melanie Madden and everyone else at The Quarto Publishing Group for making this book happen.

Thank you to my readers, especially those who told me their favorite fictional drinks when I was flailing for ideas. You guys are the reason I get to keep writing these things, and it means the world to me.

Thanks to the creators of every book, show, game, film, whatever … referenced in this book. Your creativity and genius inspire me every day, and not just in culinary ways.

ABOUT THE AUTHOR

Cassandra Reeder is an author, avid home cook, and lifetime geek. For over a decade, she has been helping other geeks and nerds all over the world make their fictional food fantasies come true at www.geekychef. com. She released her first cookbook, *The Geeky Chef Cookbook*, in 2014, and its sequel, *The Geek Chef Strikes Back*, in 2017. Cassandra currently lives and cooks in Portland, OR, with her husband, son, and a magical talking parrot.